Disciplemaking GIRLS

KATIE EDWARDS

Disciplemaking with Girls

Copyright © 2023 by Katie Edwards
Publisher: Mark Oestreicher
Managing Editor: Sarah Hauge
Cover Design and Layout: Marilee Pankratz
Creative Director: Susan Pevensie

All rights reserved. No part of this book may be reproduced in any form by any electronic or mechanical means including photocopying, recording, or information storage and retrieval without permission in writing from the author.

Scripture quotations marked (NIV) are taken from the Holy Bible, New International Version®, NIV®. Copyright © 1973, 1978, 1984, 2011 by Biblica, Inc.® Used by permission. All rights reserved worldwide.

Scripture quotations marked NLT are taken from the *Holy Bible*, New Living Translation, copyright © 1996, 2004, 2015 by Tyndale House Foundation. Used by permission of Tyndale House Publishers, Inc., Carol Stream, Illinois 60188. All rights reserved.

ISBN-13: 978-1-942145-76-9

The Youth Cartel, LLC
www.theyouthcartel.com
Email: info@theyouthcartel.com
Born in San Diego.
Printed Worldwide.

CONTENTS

PART 1: UNDERSTANDING TEENAGE GIRLS

Introduction	7
Chapter One	21
Chapter Two	35
Chapter Three	43
Chapter Four	53
Chapter Five	61

PART 2: WITH IS THE WAY

Chapter Six	73
Chapter Seven	81
Chapter Eight	99
Chapter Nine	109

PART 3: THE INGREDIENTS THAT MAKE UP A DISCIPLE

Chapter Ten	129
Chapter Eleven	147
Chapter Twelve	167
Chapter Thirteen	185

PART 4: LET'S MAKE DISCIPLES, PEOPLE!

Chapter Fourteen	197
Chapter Fifteen	205
Chapter Sixteen	221
Acknowledgements	226
Endnotes	228

For Abby
I wanted to give you what I wished someone would have given me when I was 22 and just starting out in youth ministry. I am sure you are wishing I would give you a higher salary, but you'll have to settle for these wise words instead.

Introduction

Disciplemaking with Girls

I met Allison as a sixth grader at our church's summer camp. She was eleven years old and homesick. I remember her wearing a yellow sweatsuit, a small fact that she disputes to this day, I think because it was an embarrassing-looking yellow sweatsuit. I remember that detail so vividly because it was the reason she initially caught my eye. She was sitting on a bench outside of her tent, crying. I walked over, sat beside her, and asked why she was crying. She launched into a tearful retelling of her past twenty-four hours. She told me her camp counselor had broken up with her boyfriend right before camp and therefore was emotionally unavailable to the eight sixth-grade girls in the tent. In Allison's words, "she is really sad and doesn't want to talk to us."

She went on to tell me she was feeling a little homesick and had just thrown up in the bathroom. Gotcha. The smell, the tears, the pale face, it all made sense. (Also, is there anything grosser than students in your ministry throwing up at camp? It's one of those things you didn't know you were signing up for, and you just gotta figure out a way to stay present even though you want to run away.) All this to say, she wasn't having the best week. We sat together for a while on that bench. We chatted, I worked to make her laugh, she told me about her family, and that she could sing, and then proceeded to sing for me, and I think I prayed with her? (It feels like something I would do, but I was nineteen and this was a long time ago, and I might be remembering this story with me as a super spiritual hero. But I promise the other details are accurate!)

I had no idea at the time, but that moment was the beginning of a thirty-plus year discipleship journey with Allison. It began when she was in sixth grade and it is still going today, just a few months shy of her fortieth birthday. Allison was the first student I discipled. She was the first student I wanted to "make a disciple," and I first committed myself to the discipleship process with her. I didn't fully know what I was doing, I didn't have a road map, but I knew I was called to help her fall deeper in love with Jesus and become a stronger disciple of him.

As I look back over the role I played in Allison's life, I can see some very intentional steps we took, and then a huge collection of unintentional "life together" type moments that can absolutely still fall under the "discipleship" label.

Introduction

Our time together included, in no particular order, church services, middle school small group, mission trips, camps, travelling around the world together, lunches, dinners, laughing, crying, prayer, more church, support, worship together, serving together, navigating pain and grief, questions and doubt, working together on a church staff, and the list really does go on and on. There was a lot of encouragement, prayer, letting mistakes be made, loving without expectation, loving her for her, always meeting her where she was, and trying not to say, "I told you so" but "how can I help now?" There was also lots of dyed hair and fashion choices that some might say were a mistake, but not me. I've always been her fan.

I also wasn't the only one in the discipleship process with her. I was part of a village of people who surrounded Allison: her mom, her youth pastor, two other small group leaders , and a musical worship mentor. All of us were discipling her in the ways of Jesus. The village. Every person pouring into her in different and yet equally important ways.

Allison loves Jesus. She has had a full journey so far, and yet she continues to grow as a disciple of Jesus. She is curious and is not afraid to ask questions. She is empathetic and compassionate and loves God's people well. She is a servant leader, someone who serves first and then leads from there. She is a gifted singer with a gift for ushering people into beautiful worship experiences. She is administrative and organized and creatively leads inside and outside the church with those gifts. I look at her now and I think, *Wow. I got to be a part of her story. I played a role in making her a disciple.*

Stories like that are what this book is about. Helping every girl become a strong disciple of Jesus through a deeper personal relationship with him, a village of consistent godly adult voices, and a pathway filled with intentional and unintentional practices and experiences in faith. In many ways, being part of Allison's journey and walking with her over the years gave me a road map for discipling other girls God brought into my life later. That road map is what I'll share with you in the pages ahead. I wish I had a resource like this when I first started in youth ministry. It would have saved me a lot of trial and error. Because for all of the great moments I had with Allison, I can also pinpoint some where I blew it and got it wrong. Thankfully, we serve a merciful, loving

Disciplemaking with Girls

God who covers up all our blunders with his goodness and faithfulness.

MAKING DISCIPLES OF TEENAGE GIRLS IS FOR THE BRAVE

I've believed for a long time that only the bravest people serve in ministry to teenage girls. I realize that sounds a bit dramatic, but that's fitting. I am, after all, a former teenage girl. The word *brave* also comes to mind when I think of all the women and men who discipled me when I was a teenager. I gave my life to Jesus when I was fourteen and knew *nothing* about following him. I was the first Christ-follower in my home, so I needed a lot in the way of discipleship. Oh also, did I mention I was kind of mess my freshman year of high school? I was fresh off my parents' divorce, deep wounds, hurts, grief, failing in school, and looking for love and authentic friendships without a lot of luck. There are four people who intentionally discipled me in high school. As I think now of the people who discipled me, I see them as brave, godly people who stepped right into the middle of my messy story. They pushed past my teenage angst, mess, and any fears or intimidation they felt, jumping right into helping me become a stronger disciple of Jesus. It took courage on their part, and I know it wasn't easy. I think that's why I believe disciplemaking is for the brave. This is "on the frontlines" ministry. And it's not for the faint of heart. (Yeah, I know that sounds dramatic too—I like drama.)

It's true, though. According to Barna,

> Families, churches and parachurch ministries must recognize that primary window of opportunity for effectively reaching people with the good news of Jesus' death and resurrection is during the pre-teen and teen years. It is during those years that people develop their frames of reference for the remainder of their life – especially theologically and morally. Consistently explaining and modeling truth principles for young people is the most critical factor in their spiritual development.[1]

Which paints a picture of how important it is to disciple girls in their teenage years. THIS IS WHY DISCIPLESHIP IN THIS SEASON IS SO SIGNIFICANT. (This is my last dramatic statement...in this paragraph, at least.) This is a crucial season of faith development, this is identity formation and the search for purpose, this is when adolescent development turns teenagers upside down in order to prepare them for adulthood, this is faith passed down to the next generation, and this is the crossroads season that might leave a girl on the trajectory toward a lifetime of following the way of Jesus.

That is why it requires women and men who love Jesus and are seeking to make a bold impact for the kingdom. Countercultural, loving, kind, courageous Christ-followers in daily pursuit of the King. Our girls need spiritually mature adults who are consistent, intentional, and willing to teach, guide, point them to Jesus, and help them navigate their world as a disciple. It will require buckets of time, energy, and every fruit of the Spirit, but I can't think of anything that is more worth our time. Again, this ministry isn't for the faint of heart, it's for the brave.

WHERE I AM COMING FROM
I am a youth pastor
I have been at the same church since I was thirteen—Saddleback Church in Southern California. I started serving as a small group leader in the junior high ministry when I was seventeen, interned in the same ministry when I was nineteen, and then joined the full-time staff in that same ministry when I was twenty-one. I have been there ever since (with a short departure to another church for a year). As of today, that's twenty-six years serving at my home church in a vocational capacity. I now serve as the student ministries pastor overseeing college, high school, and middle school ministries. Now, if you google my church, it has a history of being a fairly large congregation. But this is not where it began. When I first started going there, the church and various ministries were significantly smaller. When I think back, I feel like I grew up in a small youth ministry. When I was in junior high, the ministry was six students and when I was in high school, the ministry was twenty-five. The reason I am telling you this is because I think sometimes people look at where my church is now and who I am as a youth pastor now and believe that it's always been this way. That's not the case.

It's easy *and human* to sometimes feel like we can't do something because of context, numbers, and resources. I want to encourage and reassure you that everything I am going to share is not based on the setting I am in or the resources I have been given as a youth pastor.

Disciplemaking with Girls

Don't get me wrong—I am grateful for my church, my pastor, and the blessings I have. But disciplemaking isn't really based on any of that. When I discipled Allison our youth ministry and looked very different than it does today. My approach to discipleship has always been relationship centric and does not revolve around a number or a large room. If anything, the high numbers have been my biggest challenge in my setting. I am a one-on-one, small group kind of a gal, and big rooms of people cause my palms to sweat. No, really. It's the Lord's sense of humor that has me where I am.

All this to say, the church I serve has impacted me and influenced me beyond measure. But the principles I'll share are meant to be transferrable to any setting or context. There will be times when I tell stories from my church, but I am hopeful the big picture principles can find their way into your setting.

The last youth pastor-y thing you should know about me is that I love and believe in the local church. I am called to it. I love youth ministry and feel like I have the best job in the world. Over the years, many have asked me why I haven't moved on to bigger, more important platforms in our church, such as adult ministry. My response has always been the same: I believe I AM serving in the most important area of the church. There is nothing more worth my time than making disciples of the women of the next generation.

I am a mom
I've got a bunch of kids. Well, three. But there are times when that feels like "a bunch."

My husband, Ron, and I have Abby, our oldest daughter who is twenty-two, Ella, our middle daughter who is nineteen, and the baby, our eleven-year-old son, Cooper. This feels important to share with you because I cannot talk about discipleship and disciplemaking and not think about my own kids.

For Ron and me, one of our greatest desires for our kids is to see them become dedicated disciples of Jesus. We know the best life ever is a life lived with and for Jesus and we have wanted that for each of them since the first day we met. As their parents we have always understood

Introduction

our role as the primary disciplemakers, but we also knew that we were never meant to do it alone.

A few years back, when our two daughters went through our middle school and high school ministries, we experienced the blessing of partnering with the church in the discipleship process. Honestly, it was the greatest season and yet, one of the most difficult as a parent. As both a mom and a youth pastor, I have a few scars from those years. Sometimes I flash back to the eye rolls and slamming doors and stomping away and I get shivers. Sometimes I can still hear the faint sound of my daughter's voice telling me how annoying I am. Again, shivers.

All that to say, though, we made it. But not alone. We had a village of adults whose voices spoke into our teenage girls, all playing different roles in the disciplemaking process. Going through the tween and teen years with my own kids was a turning point for me. It was in this season that I had a front row seat to witness the power of the discipleship process in my own home. Watching my girls as teenagers only grew my desire to see every daughter find her way to Jesus and a life with him.

Today, I can see with a little more clarity how our role as parents and their relationships with others have shaped our girls. Over the years there have been a lot of faith ups and downs, but in hindsight I can see the series of intentional and unintentional discipleship moments with our girls that contributed to them becoming the disciples they are today. Real talk: They are both still in the discipleship process and still have their weekly faith ups and downs. I don't want you to get the impression I've got perfect angel daughters who are getting it right all of the time. They are not that, but they are my very favorite two women who walk the Earth.

SHOULD WE DEFINE SOME THINGS?
I realize there are many books and resources out there that talk about discipleship. I fully understand I am not blowing your mind with the topic here. However, I do think this conversation is always relevant and there are always new perspectives, stories, and ways to help us understand our role in this process. So, before we do anything else, I

think I should define some of the key terms and phrases we are going to talk about to make sure we are on the same page.

When I talk about a **DISCIPLE**, I am talking about a dedicated follower of Jesus who is striving to learn from him, stay close with him, and be led by him in daily life.

Whew, that feels like a tall order for teenage girls, but notice I used the word "striving." At this stage we are not working toward being a fully developed follower, we are working toward being dedicated and striving, putting girls on a trajectory toward a lifelong walk with Jesus.

When I talk about a **DISCIPLEMAKER**, I am talking about a dedicated disciple of Jesus who is striving to lead by example and live with integrity, someone who is committed to pass down the ways of Jesus to the next generation.

Again, feels like a tall order, but you will see the word "striving" again here too. Why? Well, just because the disciplemaker is further along in their journey with Jesus does not mean they will always have it all together or won't make mistakes. We are all always in the sanctification process. The word "striving" is important in both definitions.

When I talk about the **DISCIPLESHIP PROCESS**, I am talking about the process of becoming a disciple through relationships. *Relational discipleship* is the process of discipleship through which we see teenage girls become stronger disciples of Jesus.

I understand that this is a broad topic influenced and shaped by many different insights, schools of thought, beliefs, and approaches. This is just ONE way to view this conversation.

These might not be definitions or ways of thinking you have used before, but these are the terms we will use as we move ahead together.

OKAY, SO WHERE ARE WE HEADED?
The chapters ahead break down disciplemaking with girls into four parts.

Introduction

Part 1: Understanding Teenage Girls
This is a hilarious header. As I type, I am giggling. As if any of us could ever fully understand a teenage girl. That's not a burn, it's just the truth. As a former teenage girl, I feel like I can say that because I was nuts and a puzzle and awesome all at the same time. However, that's a different book. But it is important for us to understand our audience, learn as much as we can, and commit to continuing to learn as we disciple girls. These chapters will deep dive into the knowns—and call out the unknowns—of teenage girls. The more we understand, the more effective and thoughtful we can be in the disciplemaking process.

Part Two: With is the Way
If we want to see girls become strong disciples, they need mature, godly women and men to give them examples to follow and show them the way to a life with Jesus. But who are these people and where do we find them? What characteristics are crucial in someone who is going to disciple teenage girls? In these chapters, we are going to spend some time unpacking the powerful impact of relational discipleship, building a team of disciplemakers, and equipping that team to disciple teenage girls. With relationships being a key component of disciplemaking, it's worth our time to think about WHO we are asking, WHAT they will do, and HOW they will be the most effective in their role.

Part Three: The Ingredients That Make Up a Disciple
Every person is unique, but there are some crucial ingredients that help put a girl on the trajectory toward becoming a devoted disciple of Jesus. Since there is no one-size-fits-all approach, these chapters will focus on four key ingredients that we mix together to make disciples: building relationships, practice and experience, partnering with parents, and intentional rallying points for relational discipleship.

Part Four: Let's Make Disciples, People!
Content dedicated to deepening faith plays a very important role in relational discipleship. It's not the only piece, but the subjects of our conversations, the content we teach, and the ways we dive into God's Word together are all crucial pieces of disciplemaking. In these chapters we are going to unpack how to choose content, some vital elements to know about that content, and how intentional conversations can open the door to utilizing content for making disciples.

Disciplemaking with Girls

PUT EVERYTHING INTO YOUR OWN CONTEXT

I understand that we are all coming from different places and spaces. As you journey through this book, my prayer is that you would be able to take some of these pieces and implement them in your setting. The thought of your girls becoming stronger disciples of Jesus just warms my heart. I hope this book encourages you, inspires you, gives you courage, and leaves you with some practical starting points for discipling teenage girls.

Okay, are you ready? Let's make some disciples, people!

Part One: UNDERSTANDING TEENAGE GIRLS

Disciplemaking with Girls

THE PUZZLE OF TEENAGE GIRLS

I like doing puzzles, and yet I kind of hate doing puzzles. I love the process of putting pieces together to create something bigger. It's fun to look at the picture on the box and then take the time to construct that picture, one piece at a time. And there is something that is so dang satisfying about a completed puzzle. You just feel like you accomplished something huge. But where I get stuck, and when I kind of hate puzzles, is the beginning. The beginning is the worst. You know, that part when you dump the box of puzzle pieces on the table and all of them land haphazardly in a big mess of colors and shapes? I hate it. I typically sit and stare at the pile for a good long while, a little overwhelmed at how I might make sense of the mess.

The turning point typically comes once I start moving the puzzle pieces around for the first time. I begin by searching for edges, grouping colors together, and finding parts of the main picture. I start making sense of how the pieces fit together. The key is referring to the picture on the box. The picture gives me the information I need to start organizing the pieces. Without it I would be lost. It acts as a road map to the end result, which, of course, is the finished puzzle.

In the pages ahead I want to give you the "picture on the box" for the puzzle of teenage girls. A guide that helps us get to our desired end result: devoted disciples of Jesus.

I believe the discipleship process with teenage girls is like working on a beautiful yet complicated 5,000-piece puzzle. You open the box, dump out the pieces, and embark on a journey with a lot of unknowns ahead. But when you start to move the pieces around, what starts as a pile on the table gradually begins to take shape into something wonderful.

The more we understand about teenage girls, the more effective we will be in the discipleship process. While we can't understand 100% of what makes a girl tick, there are things that will help us gain a better understanding of how they are wired, how they are developing, what they are up against, and how culture is shaping them. I also believe that when we take the time to grow our understanding of teenage girls, our expectations adjust, our levels of frustration are lowered, our empathy grows, and we gain insight on some of the "why" questions we ask.

Understanding Teenage Girls

In a book about discipleship, it might seem strange to camp out here for a minute and take the time to understand girls from this perspective. But, trust me, it's worth your time. More often than not, teenagers are misunderstood. As the people called, chosen, or appointed to work with teenage girls, we should make it at least part of our mission to be the ones who work to understand.

Chapter One:
Development and Discipleship

When I tell people about my vocation, I am met with a lot of similar responses. It goes something like this:

Me: "I serve in student ministry at my church."
Other person: "Well, good for you!" Or, "Well, bless your heart" (older generations or people from the South). Or, "I could never do that!" Or, "*GOD BLESS YOU.*"

I always giggle at these responses, because honestly, I get it. The perception of teenage girls is that they are straight-up crazy. But, if you were experiencing what was going on inside the mind, body, and emotions of a teenager, you would be crazy too. In fact, you were crazy once—you've just blocked it out. Seriously, take a moment and try to remember being a teenager. Are you having flashbacks to how terrible puberty was? Does your mind race toward awkward moments and embarrassing encounters? I immediately flash back to walking into the boys' locker room on the first day of seventh grade. I was lost, and *I thought* I was walking into the girls' locker room (thank you Los Alisos Middle School for your terrible attempt at clear signage). It was a scarring moment in my adolescence and yet, I can't really remember exactly what happened. Why? BECAUSE IT WAS TERRIBLE AND I DON'T WANT TO REMEMBER. I digress.

As we move into adulthood, we slowly distance ourselves from the roller coaster of adolescence. We only remember so much and our empathy will only take us so far. So, it's important to dive into this area to build a more robust understanding of what's happening in teenagers'

Disciplemaking with Girls

bodies and brains. If we are out to make disciples, we need to know what we are working with before we begin.

P.S. I do not think we need to become experts in the physiology of teenagers, but I do think having some level of understanding in this area points us toward places to offer encouragement, helps us to extend grace, adjusts our expectations as leaders, and helps challenge our thinking to shape and inform how we do what we do.

THE WOBBLE, THEN THE CRASH

Have you ever played Jenga? The tower of wooden pieces is set and then one by one you take pieces from the bottom and place them on the top. First person to topple the Jenga loses. I like to think of an adolescent girl as the Jenga tower. (By now you know for sure that I am a youth pastor since my first two teenage girl illustrations are connected to games.)

Girls start out as a solid tower. As they move toward adolescence, pieces in their physiology start to change. When they reach age eleven or twelve, the tower starts to wobble. (You know that moment in Jenga when the tower wobbles, right? Everyone holds their breath and doesn't make a move because they know something is coming.) As a parent and a youth pastor, I know this wobbly anticipation. A few more pieces move around and then, bam, girls hit age twelve or thirteen and we see the tower topple. Now, in Jenga this means you lose, but with girls, this "topple" is a positive and wonderful thing. YAY for adulthood!! This is where the pathway toward becoming an adult and, more importantly, the journey to adult faith, begins. I often tell parents that this is the point where we stop raising kids and begin to raise adults. (That statement also freaks out every parent I say it to.) But it's true, the way we walk with teenagers in this process that begins with early adolescence is what helps put them on a trajectory toward becoming a lifelong follower of Jesus.

When adolescent development begins, girls enter an extremely normal yet layered stage of life. They begin to rebuild the Jenga, this time with abstract thinking and new brain functions included in the construction. This stage also comes with the emergence of new emotions, recognition of different perspectives or viewpoints,

Development and Discipleship

the development of sexual organs and sexuality, the formation of a system of values, more personal independence, an increasing distance from family and a greater importance of peers, and the emergence of problem solving. NBD, right?

Basically, as kids move through adolescence, their brains, bodies, and emotions go through major changes, and they are moving from pandemonium to precision. Chaos to clarity.

When this change begins, it can feel like a crash. Things that were previously learned or mastered somehow seem lost in this stage. But the truth is, nothing is lost, it's just jumbled up a little bit to prepare for the maturing process ahead.

And just a reminder. This is EVERY girl. No one escapes this process. (That sounded dark, but it's true.)

DRAMA OR DEVELOPMENT?

There are many pieces to adolescent development. There are also many books and resources devoted to this topic. I think I've read at least ten on brain development alone. Since we only have a few short pages together on this, I am going to give you a snapshot of five areas of adolescent development and how they relate to discipleship. We are going to focus on the pieces that come up most often in my ministry to girls, which are cognitive, social, emotional, physical, and spiritual development.

Every girl hits these layers of development in a different order and at different times. I wish there were a methodical path, but there isn't. We know what is *in* the pathway, but each girl's experience is different. This is one of the reasons why a lot of people use the words "drama" or "dramatic" to describe teenage girls. Often, it's not drama, and girls are not being dramatic. It's just that their bodies and minds are advancing faster than they can keep up with and that causes inward and outward responses that can be misdiagnosed as "DRAMA." It's easier for adults to call something drama than it is to pull back and reflect on why a girl is acting or speaking in a certain way. More often than not, what we're looking at is *development*, not drama.

Disciplemaking with Girls

Okay, let's jump into these five areas of development and how they relate to discipleship.

PHYSICAL DEVELOPMENT
Physical development refers to what is happening on the inside and the outside simultaneously. Some things are easy to spot: pimples, voice changes, and growth spurts. Others are not as easy to see: puberty, development of sexual organs, and increased appetite and sleep. These things may seem like nothing more than physical changes, but physical development shapes worth, perception of self, insecurities, and comparison, and can cause stress, worry, and anxiety at deep levels. To an adult a pimple is just a pimple. But to a teenage girl, a pimple is the end of days.

The markers: You will see these physical markers sometime between the ages of ten and sixteen. Increase in hormones, growth spurts, height and body shape changes, sexual organs develop, appetite changes/increases, need for sleep increases, menstruation begins, body odor and body hair come on the scene, breasts develop, and so much more. A lot is happening inside and outside the body.

The inner dialogue: *Everyone is looking at my pimple. Everyone is probably talking about the way I look. I wish I were taller. I wish I were shorter. How do I hide these boobs? Why don't I have boobs? Why does my whole body hurt? I think I am sick. I wish I were skinnier. Why does my nose take up my whole face? Why did I pick this outfit? Does anyone notice my outfit?*

The perceived drama: Tears over a bad haircut. No longer fitting in a favorite shirt from fourth grade. Getting your period for the first time. A girl's reactions to these moments can make her seem dramatic. But when you don't feel good physically, emotions and actions often follow suit. It's not drama when your mind and body feel like they are under siege. Girls lash out, they are unfiltered, and they show emotions. It might not be drama, it could just be physical development.

The fight: At this point, girls are up against comparison and confusion. They are constantly comparing themselves to everyone around them and rarely taking the time to find out if their thoughts are accurate. The comparison game opens up lanes for false narratives and false beliefs about themselves. There is also a lot of confusion. It is confusing to experience something physically but have no idea what you are actually feeling or why. When comparison and confusion hold hands, it can be a fight to survive.

The discipleship process: How does physical development impact the discipleship process? There are so many ways we can be intentional as youth workers in this area. We can affirm character and help girls focus on who God made them to be. We can remind girls of their significance and that they were made on purpose for God's purpose. We can remind them often of how God sees them and that their identity can be found in him. We can comfort with presence and prayer and God's promises when they are feeling physically out of sorts. We can encourage when they are caught up in comparing themselves to others. We can reassure when things feel confusing, reminding them that they are created by God.

By growing our awareness of physical development, we can be more effective in our discipleship role.

EMOTIONAL DEVELOPMENT
Girls are sorting through a range of new emotions and what to do with them. As girls are introduced to new emotions, they feel them… *deeply*. Emotional development makes me think of baby rattlesnakes. Baby rattlesnakes are more dangerous than adult snakes because they can't control their venom. When they bite you, they just keep going with no control. Bite – venom – bite – venom – bite – venom. Emotional development has that baby rattlesnake vibe. Sometimes the emotions come tumbling out with no control. No rhyme or reason. The emotional pendulum swings hard and fast, leaving most innocent bystanders scratching their heads and asking, "what just happened?"

The markers: You will see these markers of emotional development sometime between the ages of eleven and eighteen: masking emotions when they feel confused, benefits that come from talking about feelings and why they feel what they do, arguing or debates as a way of seeking relief from a feeling or emotion, lying to cover up something they are feeling, advancement of sense of humor, a tendency to overcommit and overschedule, and lots of extremes. Ups and downs at different levels of intensity.

The inner dialogue: *I'm sad, I'm happy, I hate you, I love you. You are my favorite, wait no, don't talk to me ever again. I'm tired, but wait, at a sleepover I could stay up all night. Leave me alone, but don't leave me alone, stay close…no wait, go away. I'm so stressed, but yes, I can babysit, no problem. I can't handle one more thing, but yes, I can do the whole group project by myself. Meltdown. Tears. No one sees me. I love playing basketball, but also my parents are getting divorced.*

What? Ahhhh, calm down, baby rattlesnake!!

The perceived drama: I can remember sitting with my seventh grade daughter at breakfast one morning. She asked for pancakes, so I made pancakes. I set the plate in front of her and two minutes later she was crying. When I asked why, she just looked up at me (fully in tears) and said, "I don't know." I asked her again if she knew what she was feeling and she said (still fully in tears), "I don't want these pancakes." I turned around and smiled to myself knowing pancakes were not the issue, she simply felt something she couldn't identify.

She was desperate to pin her emotions on something tangible and the easiest way to find relief was to blame the pancakes. Most girls are looking for something tangible to point to when it comes to their emotions. These can be mistaken for "dramatic" moments. But oftentimes, it's not drama, it's emotional development.

The fight: When it comes to emotions, I believe there are two things at war in a teenage girl. The fight is between where to lean in and feel emotions and where to let go and not let emotions control her. Emotions are good, created by God, and we should encourage exploring them. It's healthy to really feel things and let those feelings hold a place in our day-to-day lives. But there are also times when emotions take over the head and the heart, leading and guiding when they shouldn't. Emotions can sometimes create a sense of truth that isn't real. This inner battle is ongoing throughout adolescence, but with time and practice the fight becomes a little easier.

Development and Discipleship

The discipleship process: How does emotional development impact the discipleship process? There are so many ways we as youth workers can be intentional in this area. We can connect the dots between God and our emotions, helping girls understand they were created in the image of God. He feels things and so do we. We can show girls how our emotions are linked with the fruit of the Spirit. We can encourage girls to talk to Jesus to help discern what emotions they, and we, are feeling. We can help girls practice expressing emotions in our faith, such as through prayer, silence and solitude, and singing.

By growing our awareness about emotional development, we can be more effective in our discipleship role.

RELATIONAL/SOCIAL DEVELOPMENT

As peer relationships begin to shift and take center stage, so begins a real good time with teenage girls. That was sarcasm. Honestly, I believe relational and social development is very difficult to navigate. It's a four-way tug o' war between friendships and dating, status and social media. Girls are looking for a few good, loving, authentic friends, but often, they end up settling for anyone with a heartbeat. Social media becomes a central place of connection and communication with varying degrees of depth. Girls are desperately looking to feel known and sometimes settle for social status to fill that void. And dating. Hmmmm...what can I say about middle school and high school dating? I mean, it's tough. Let's just leave it at that. There are a lot of misunderstandings, unexpressed feelings, cutthroat decisions, and sometimes we see multiple versions of the same girl in her various social settings.

The markers: You will see these social markers sometime between the ages of eleven and eighteen. Relationships constantly shift and change. Friendships move from situational (kids from the school classroom, children of parents' friends) to affinity-based (sports, hobbies, things they have in common). The desire to negotiate rules in accordance with social activities. The desire to build a social circle made up of people and various social media platforms. Thinking a lot about how everyone perceives them. Looking to increase independence. Searching for belonging. Constantly thinking about where they fit with people and where they fit in the world.

Disciplemaking with Girls

The inner dialogue: *I wish I had one really good friend. I wish I had more than just one friend. Why didn't I get invited to that? I don't want to invite her. She's changed so much since eighth grade. Is that post about me? I am seventeen, why do I have a curfew? Why don't my parents like my boyfriend? My boyfriend is perfect. I have no one to talk to. Does anyone really know me? Why did that picture only get fifty likes? I like him, I wonder if he likes me? He doesn't like me, I wonder what's wrong with me?*

The perceived drama: Changing friendships and constant shifts in alliances can feel very intense. Social development reminds me of being in a dressing room at a clothing store. Girls are constantly trying on different friendships until they find the one or two that fit best. This can seem cutthroat or harsh at times, especially when it comes to childhood friends, but it is the reality of socially maturing. Friendships are changing every day, girls are rotating social media handles, and their daily crushes can give the impression of drama, but honestly, it's just part of the process.

The fight: Loneliness is the major obstacle girls are up against here. A girl will stick it out in toxic friendships long term just so she doesn't feel so alone. She will run with a pack just to feel part of group, even if she doesn't feel a genuine connection. Loneliness is running rampant among teenagers today, so settling for any friends feels better than not having any friends at all. This is a daily fight because peer influences are so significant.

The discipleship process: There are so many ways we can be intentional as youth workers in this area. We can help girls understand authentic fellowship and how to seek out the friends who are part of it. We can have conversations around what it looks like to pursue a dating relationship that honors God. We can have conversations around integrity and how that translates into our daily life. We can start small groups and work to create spaces for students to find authentic belonging. Girls need older generations of men and woman pouring into them. We can create spaces for our girls and adults (other than mom and dad) to mentor and guide and disciple.

Development and Discipleship

By growing our awareness of social development, we can be more effective in our discipleship role.

COGNITIVE DEVELOPMENT

This might sound like the most boring of the development areas, but honestly, I think it's exciting. The brain of every girl goes through a maturing process over the course of adolescence. It starts around age twelve and the brain doesn't fully mature until age twenty-five. This is the second most rapid season of brain development in a girl's lifetime, with the first being birth to two years old. This maturing process includes the construction of cognitive and emotional control networks and an active reorganization and growth of the prefrontal cortex, which is basically the brain's CEO. With these changes come many wonderful things that help teenage girls turn the corner toward adult faith.

The markers: You will see these cognitive markers sometime between the ages of twelve and twenty-five. The rise of self-awareness and self-evaluation. Connecting dots from one concept to the next in order to form a viewpoint. The shift from concrete thought to abstract thought. The development of problem solving, coping, and organizational skills. The development of the prefrontal cortex.

The inner dialogue: *I don't know what I think about that. Let me tell you every thought I have about that. Why do I believe that? Why do they believe that? Why do we think so differently? What do I think about that? Was I wrong before? This is right. This is wrong. This is right and wrong. I am not sure what is right and what is wrong.*

The perceived drama: What could be more dramatic than your brain changing?

As girls are learning and growing in so many areas simultaneously, you might see them change their minds, make rash decisions, or give you a blank stare. I think about this often when I am leading my girls small group Bible study. There are moments when I ask a question, and when I look around the circle I am met with a lot of blank stares. I swear, nothing makes me feel more insecure as a leader than blank looks on the faces of my students. But what I realized (or at least what I secretly hope to be true) is that nine times out of ten they are just working things out in their minds. Their thoughts might be wandering from a spark in the conversation, or they are trying to think through the answer, or their brains just straight up don't know what to do. One girl actually lay down on the floor during small group last week. I assume her brain just hurt real bad during our discussion. Keep in mind that a slew of rash decisions, apathy, or a constantly changing mind can sometimes be mistaken for drama. But it's not—it's cognitive development.

The fight: Girls are up against a lot when it comes to learning to problem solve, cope, and share opinions in the teenage world. Honestly, I believe the fight in this arena is exhaustion. Every girl's brain is working overtime forming and performing all of its new functions. The brain never shuts down—and when it is maturing, that can be exhausting. A few days ago, Cassie from my small group walked in the room and plopped down on the couch. I asked her how her week had been. She looked at me and said, "My brain hurts." I laughed a little, and then asked, "Tell me why your brain hurts, Cassie?" She went on to talk about school and friendships and a fight she got in with her mom. She also talked about a moment when she had to make a choice and didn't know what to do. After she was done talking, my brain hurt too. In every situation she has new functions developing and then being tested. It's no wonder she was mentally drained from the overtime her brain was working. I imagine it's tough to feel like you are in a fight everyday with your own brain (I can't remember, I blocked it out).

The discipleship process: How does cognitive development impact the discipleship process? There are so many ways we can be intentional as youth workers in this area. We are on a journey with girls. We can let go of the pressure to cram everything into just one season—we have time. We can give space for processing and critical thinking when it comes to reading Scripture or developing personal faith. We can teach them where problem solving, coping strategies, and emotions fit in their relationship with Jesus. We can get comfortable with silence and not answering all their questions. We can show them how to ask God their big questions, to seek out clarity in Scripture, and how to wrestle with having faith when there is no answer.

Development and Discipleship

By growing our awareness of cognitive development, we can be more effective in our discipleship role.

SPIRITUAL DEVELOPMENT

As abstract thinking kicks in, the concrete nature of faith begins to crumble. Not to worry, this is super normal and crucial to spiritual development. When critical thinking, doubt, problem-solving, and decision-making collide, it only makes belief and faith stronger. Whether a girl grew up in the church or is jumping into a relationship with Jesus for the first time as a teenager, this process of spiritual development affects everyone. Girls will either question what they currently believe or they will question belief in general. It can be easy to panic when doubts arise, but don't. We *want* girls to wrestle with what they believe. A faith that is wrestled with is a faith that is owned.

The markers: You will see these spiritual development markers sometime between the ages of twelve and twenty-five. Deconstruction of childhood faith and reconstruction of adult faith. Growing independence in spiritual disciplines. Increased desire to find purpose. Increased desire to find their place in the church body. Questioning belief and asking lots of "why" questions. Growing understanding of relationship vs. religion. Growing desire for depth and spiritual maturity.

The inner dialogue: *I believe in Jesus, but why am I a Christian? I believe in the Bible, but how do I know the Bible is true? Why does God allow bad things to happen to the best people? I want to go deeper. I don't think God can use me; I am not really good at anything. Why am I here? I wish Jesus was standing right here with me. I fall asleep every time I pray, does that make me a bad person? Is Jesus disappointed in me because I don't read my Bible every day?*

The perceived drama: Spiritual growth is messy. "Messy" might not be the adjective we hope for here, but it's a perfect word to describe a teenage girl's journey to becoming a stronger disciple of Jesus. There are ups and downs, moments of maturity and growth, and then setbacks through choices and behaviors. One minute a girl can look like the most dedicated follower of Jesus and the next minute she can seem so far away. All of this can leave us youth workers feeling like we

Disciplemaking with Girls

have whiplash, or maybe aren't even cut out for discipleship. But hang in there. It's not drama, it's spiritual development.

The fight: The process of refining faith is tough. When our girls are questioning everything they believe, they often feel like they're on shaky ground. It's easy for them to feel guilty or ashamed when asking questions about their relationship with Jesus. When they're experiencing doubt, their questions, at times, can seem to them like a betrayal. Sometimes our girls feel like they're at war with themselves. The fight here for teenage girls is between submission to childhood faith and permission to explore all of the new facets of adult faith. It takes courage to question what you've always known to be true in order to understand that truth at a deeper level.

The discipleship process: How does spiritual development impact the discipleship process? I think the better question is, isn't discipleship itself the spiritual development process? Yes. Yes, it is. Spiritual development and all of its accompanying messiness is the process of becoming a stronger disciple of Jesus. How does knowing this help us as youth workers to be intentional with our students?

We can make space for girls to question and create safe spaces for doubt. When we understand that their questions are part of the natural development process, deconstruction and reconstruction aren't as scary. Experiencing and moving through doubt is essential to having a deep, long-term relationship with Jesus.

We can give girls opportunities to practice following Jesus daily and experience moments with him. We can navigate the ups and downs of faith alongside our girls, knowing that our encouraging presence could make all the difference when a girl is wavering. We can show up often. In the sea of voices girls are listening to, they need consistent godly voices giving them guidance.

By growing our awareness in area of spiritual development, we can be more effective in our discipleship role.

LAST THOUGHTS
Oh man, that felt like drinking through the adolescent development

firehose. Here's the deal. There is so much more to know on this topic, but I wanted to give you a basic overview and connect a few dots between development and discipleship. It was a lot, but I think learning about these topics is completely worth it. When we better understand our girls' development processes, it grows our empathy, grows the grace we extend, brings thoughtfulness to our approach, and helps us to be more effective guides in our girls' discipleship journey.

Chapter Two:
Girl World Part I: The Essentials

"YOU ARE HERE"
When you visit an amusement park, it is standard protocol to grab a map of the park on your way through the front gates. As you take your first steps in, you examine the map to see where everything is and begin to plot out the day ahead. The most helpful marker on the map is the "YOU ARE HERE" icon. It gives you a starting point and helps get you where you want to go. Of course, you *could* figure out where you are without it, by why would you want to?

"Girl world" is a real place. Well, not a literal place, but it *feels* like a real place. Like any new territory that might seem strange at first, it's nice to have a map to get the lay of the land. As we continue to put together the pieces of the puzzle of teenage girls, a trip to girl world feels necessary. Girl world is a magical planet with ever changing scenery, cultural influences, and what sometimes feels like a very confusing set of unspoken rules. We just learned about the physiology of a girl. The changes that happen in adolescent development happen to every girl without exception. But there are things that influence a girl outside of development that also deserve our attention. These are the factors that inform and contribute to the world a girl lives in—things like peer influences, the surrounding community of adults, culture, generational markers, technology, and world issues, just to name a few.

Over the next few chapters, we are going to travel around girl world to get a snapshot of things we can expect to encounter with the girls we are discipling. This map might spark ideas of how we can be even more intentional in our discipleship journey. In exploring girl world I'll cover some generalizations, but I will also pinpoint many specific

Discipletmaking with Girls

interactions with teenage girls that will show how these bigger ideas connect to specific kids.

As a longtime youth pastor and as a mom, I have longed for a roadmap or handbook that would help me understand more about teenage girls. This chapter covers things I wish I had known sooner. It would have helped me be more intentional earlier in my ministry and in my parenting journey. I hope it will help you.

Okay, here we go: entering GIRL WORLD now.

Shatter stereotypes
Today's girl is a unique combination of an endless array of traits and interests. Shopping, makeup, and pink? Girls might like those things, but they might also like to hike, hoop, and shoot guns. It's time to shatter any stereotypes of what a typical girl is. There is no one-size-fits-all and there is NOTHING that describes every girl. Girls are like onions with many layers of likes, dislikes, hobbies, passions, and preferences. Let me give you some examples:

- Elle's favorite color is brown, she likes classic rock, she sews and embroiders, she hates every pastel color, she lifts weights, and she has a quick wit. She cuts and dyes her own hair, and she will put you to shame in any video game competition.
- Hannah loves soccer, basketball, and volleyball. She is the president of the Fellowship of Christian Athletes at her high school and she loves to sing (she's not great at it, she just likes it). She is kind and introverted and loves country music.
- Abigail is great at math, loves her puppy, loves purple (too much in my opinion), and is most comfortable in baggy clothes. There is no occasion on which she doesn't feel empowered to wear an oversized hoodie, baggy jeans, and Converse high tops. She would only wear a dress if you paid her cash money. She babysits and serves in the kid's ministry at our church, and I think she might be a pastor someday.
- Casey is headed off to do ROTC at college. She loves to hike, she is competitive, she is loud (SO loud), she has a great sense of humor, and she is fiercely loyal. She makes jewelry in her spare time, doesn't

wear a stitch of makeup, and is always dressed in whatever is the latest trend. Seriously, she is a walking runway model.

All this to say, every girl is a unique creation of God. Whatever stereotypes about girls have been ingrained within you, it's time to let them go. We need to approach each girl with a genuine interest in getting to know her, rather than expecting her to be something that fits a stereotype. And while we are at it, let go of the phrase "for a girl." You know, "you throw well, for a girl." I had a boss once who told me I was "a great leader, for a female." While the word "female" *is* one of my descriptors, it has nothing to do with why I am good leader. There are so many other things that contribute to my leadership ability! Let's work on saying, "Wow you have a really strong throwing arm" or "You are a really great leader" or "You are so smart." The end.

Again, we want to meet each girl in the middle of where *she* is, celebrating the girl she was made to be and all of the unique, specific things that make her…well, her.

The myth of maturity

With the rapid evolution of technology in society, information about any given topic is at our fingertips. With all of that available to them, teenage girls can sometimes present as more mature than they actually are. With increased knowledge and more awareness of the larger world around them, girls may appear to have more wisdom and life experience than they did in previous generations—but again, this does not mean they are actually more mature than the teens who came before them. Maturity is still a slow process and it takes time. According to recent research, the maturing process actually seems to be slowing a bit with younger generations.

Jean Twenge, author of *iGen*, discussed this in an article in *USA Today*:

> Today's teens are on a slow road to adulthood, putting off risky behaviors from drinking to sex, but also delaying jobs, driving, dating and other steps towards independence, according to a new study based on 40 years of survey data.

Disciplemaking with Girls

> Compared to teens from the 70s, 80s and 90s, today's teens "are taking longer to engage in both the pleasures and the responsibilities of adulthood," said Jean Twenge, professor of psychology at San Diego State University and the lead author on the study published Tuesday in the journal Child Development.
>
> "The whole developmental pathway has slowed down," she said, with today's 18-year-olds living more like 15-year-olds once did.
>
> But Twenge and her co-author Heejung Park, assistant professor of psychology at Bryn Mawr College, say the trends all point in the same direction – a slowing of teen development that matches a well-documented slowing of young adult development. While people in their early 20s now often act more like teens, young teens often act more like children, Twenge said.[2]

The articles I've read around this topic are all in agreement that the process of maturing to adulthood has slowed down in recent years. Now, we might celebrate some of that slowing, but we need to look at the outcomes of maturity having reached an all-time "slow." Milestones such as getting your driver's license and moving out of your parents' house, huge markers of maturity, seem to be occurring at later ages than they once did, and sometimes they don't occur at all. Why is this important? Because becoming a devoted disciple of Jesus is a maturing process. The discipleship process itself is one that puts a girl on a path toward spiritual maturity. It helps for youth workers and other adults to understand that students might be able to obtain knowledge about their faith quickly, but that doesn't translate to them being spiritually mature. Girls today are able to look up answers to big questions, read blogs, listen to podcasts, google a billion commentaries, listen to sermons from pastors all over the globe, and so on. There is a wealth of knowledge available, and they know exactly how to access it. They can fill up their heads with all sorts of information, but the process of maturing as a Christ-follower takes a lot more time than a google search does. As youth workers we need to consistently remind ourselves that just because a student knows the answers to our questions does not mean that those answers have taken root in their heart. They say knowledge is power, but I disagree with that

Girl Word Part I: The Essentials

when it comes to discipleship. Knowledge is good, but the journey to understanding what that knowledge means to us is greater.

A myriad of voices shaping her worldview

Have you ever thought about how many voices speak into the life of a teenage girl? I love lists, so let's make one.

- Parents (includes stepparent, foster parent, guardian)
- Grandparents
- Extended family
- Close friends/friends
- Acquaintances
- Coach/extracurricular instructor
- Teachers (five+ per semester)
- Small group leader
- Pastor/youth pastor
- Social media "friends"/influencers
- Work supervisor (if they have a job)

Now, I know this exact list doesn't apply to every girl, but they most likely have a significant chunk of these people speaking into their lives. Look it over and think about these voices for a minute. How do these voices help girls shape a worldview, a choice, a hard decision, or a relationship? How do these voices contribute to worry or anxiety? How do these voices contribute to how a girl sees herself? How many of these voices are encouraging or loving or kind? How many of these voices are pointing a girl to talk to Jesus or read God's Word for encouragement?

The answer could be *all of them*, or the answer could be *a few*. The truth is every girl has many voices shaping her. But no one voice is shaping every area, and who knows how many voices are championing her becoming a stronger disciple of Jesus. You might be in partnership with family in that pursuit or you might be in partnership with no one. As a youth worker, these are important things to keep in the back of your mind. Your voice is important. The truth you share, the encouragement you give, the ways you point a girl to her relationship with Jesus, how you help her connect with the deeper disciplines of faith, all of these things might only come from you—though of course we hope that we are one of many positive voices in a girl's life. When we understand this, it helps us to be just a little bolder and a little more courageous in how we disciple. It's also important to remember that there are many of voices competing for a girl's devotion. Voices from social media, voices focused on achievement, and voices of peers all help to shape a girl's reality and perspective and worldview and faith.

In a world of many voices, how can we consistently and boldly use our voices to point girls to God's voice, perspective, and truth for their lives?

Survival mode

Most years I find myself leading an eighth grade girls small group Bible study. It is my favorite age in the world. I've led girls in every year between seventh and twelfth grade, but for some reason eighth grade has always been my very favorite year of youth ministry. My small group this year meets on Tuesday nights in the home of one of the girls in the group. This past week, I arrived a little early to get things set up, and in walked Lera. She's fourteen, hugs big, and is joyful and smiley, the kind of girl who always bounces into the room. You know the type, right? They score a "Tigger" on the Winnie the Pooh personality test. That's Lera. But on this particular night, she walked in the room with a sad expression. She took a seat on the couch and just seemed down. I asked her how her day was, and she burst into tears.

In these moments I never know what is coming next. In my mind I am thinking, *Are you physically hurt? Did you fail a math test? Did someone hurt you? Do you have a zit?* (Thinking about development, you really just never know.) She looked up me with big crocodile tears in her eyes and said, "I don't have any friends." Ugh. Gut punch. I put my arm around Lera and asked her to tell me about it.

She said she doesn't have any real friends at school. Every day she shows up and doesn't know who she is going to sit with at lunch or if there will be anyone to walk to class with. Her group of friends from seventh grade is icing her out and she doesn't know why. Every day she is working up the courage just to show up to school. Honestly, I get it. Imagine how it would feel, walking into a space day after day not knowing if you will thrive or just have to survive. I would cry too.

Not every girl has the same issue as Lera, but I do believe every girl is trying to survive something each day. It's dog-eat-dog out there in girl world, people! Just kidding. Kind of. It can definitely feel that way to a teenage girl. There are so many areas where girls can struggle: academics, sports, friendships, dating relationships, or much more.

Even the girls who seem like they have it all together actually don't. I've met with girls who are super popular but feel incredibly lonely. I've met with girls who are super smart, but struggle with crippling anxiety. On the outside, it can seem like they are thriving, but internally? They are working to survive, just like everyone else.

What does this have to do with discipleship? Maybe it helps us to bring gentleness and empathy to our conversations. Maybe it helps us to be on the lookout for where girls are struggling and point them toward relief and reassurance in their relationship with Jesus. Maybe it reminds us to put our arm around a girl who is just trying to survive something. Maybe in that moment we don't need to say anything at all. Our presence reminds her that she's not alone. It's an embrace in the name of Jesus.

LAST THOUGHTS
We are entering God's work in progress.

When I first got into youth ministry, I remember thinking, "I can't wait to share *all the things* with the girls God entrusts to me." I had a list of lessons, learnings, and Bible stuff to impart to every girl. This wasn't a bad thing, but it wasn't good either. I had an agenda a mile long and hadn't really stopped to think about the girls themselves, or that I might be entering into God's work in progress. I don't fault young Katie Edwards; she was just doing what most adults do when they think about leading teenagers: talk everything *they* think is important and let that lead and guide the discipleship process.

What I have learned over the years is that every girl is living in God's big story for her life, and I *GET* to play a part in that. My role is to

Disciplemaking with Girls

participate in the discipleship process with God and what he is doing in the life of every girl entrusted to me. Sometimes that means setting the agenda with his guidance, and sometimes that means setting aside the agenda because God is leading in another direction or wants to do something different than I do. Ultimately my role is to listen and be led by God's Spirit at work within me. He will always lead me in a way that will help me in turn lead my girls the way they need. Whew, that was a mouthful. Basically, his leading will always result in his best for girls in my ministry. As we disciple teenage girls, understanding that they were made by God, in his image, for his glory and his purpose, gives us perspective on the role we are meant to play in their lives and the ultimate plan we are a part of.

Chapter Three:
Girl World Part 2: The Search

I lose something literally every day. My glasses, my keys, my purse, my watch. I am notorious for setting things down and not remembering where that spot was. I tell myself things like, *I am going to put this here so I won't forget.* And then…I forget. I am always running about eight minutes behind, so I am typically panicking by the time I'm looking for my keys. I go through all the motions: retracing my steps, thinking out loud, chastising myself, asking every member of my family if they've seen them, and so on. I really hate those moments. But then relief comes when I ultimately find what I'm looking for, and life can resume. I love that feeling.

My daily panic and desperation to find small things is nothing compared to the daily search teenage girls are on. Girls are seeking answers that help them build the foundation of who they are, answers that will help guide and inform decisions, actions, feelings, and direction. The hope is they would build the foundation of their life on Jesus. I realize that reads as kind of idealistic, but really, imagine what could be possible if a girl put Jesus at the center of the search. That's what I want to strive for.

SEARCHING FOR IDENTITY
Who am I? It's a question every teenage girl asks at one point or another. They are seeking identity that's rooted in something meaningful. The search is intense and can even feel desperate, because identity informs everything. When we know who we are, there is literally no corner of life that isn't affected by it. Imagine how out of sorts you'd feel if you didn't know who you were.

Disciplemaking with Girls

Girls often answer the question "Who am I?" by thinking about the various categories that describe them.

Who I am is based on…
- How I look
- Who I hang out with
- Who I am attracted to
- Where I come from or the community I live in
- What I can do
- What I have
- My image on social media
- My culture or heritage

I am a basketball player.
I live in a wealthy neighborhood.
I am a 5.0 student. (Yes, that is possible.)
I am sunshinegirl1212.
I am Cody's girlfriend.

While these might be valid or positive parts of a girl's life, they do not define who she is.

Where can we jump in and help in the search?
The world is unsteady and imperfect, so seeking identity apart from God will always lead to restlessness. As we disciple girls in the way of Jesus, we get to help them find their identity in something steady and perfect. Connecting the dots between who I am AND *whose I am*. Helping girls understand that they were made in the image of God to be loved by him and to be adopted into his family. Defining ourselves in our relationship with him and allowing that relationship to inform every corner of life. *Who am I? I am a child of God. I am a child of God who plays basketball. I am child of God who is student body president. I am child of God who is Cody's girlfriend.* (I have no idea who Cody is, it's just a name that is stuck in my head for some reason. I am sure he is really nice.) We GET to be a part of our girls' search, pointing them toward the discovery of their true identity in Christ and the richness that brings.

Girl World Part 2: The Search

SEARCHING FOR PURPOSE
This could be a tough one to wrap your head around due to the fact that you probably see girls do many things for seemingly no reason at all. But it's true, girls are searching for their purpose. They're asking questions like, *Why did God make me this way? What makes me special? What can I do? Why me? Why not me? Why am I here? Why am I doing this?* Girls have a strong desire to understand their unique wiring, their unique attributes, their unique story, and how that uniqueness can contribute to the world around them. Just look at the volume of personality tests, quizzes, and assessments out there. There's a strong desire to discover more about how we as individuals are wired. What fruit are you and what does that say about you? What is your perfect job? What celebrity are you most like? (Please know that I have taken every single one of these quizzes.) The motivation behind assessments and quizzes is discovery: discovery of passions, talents, and desires that give insight into what makes us tick, what we are good at, or what we love to do. Girls are searching for purpose and it's in the discovery process that it can be found.

The search slows when it hits speed bumps in the forms of comparison, peer influence, and social contexts. These are all moments when a girl's focus shifts toward trying to fit in versus leaning into uniqueness. These bumps don't end the process, but they do slow it down and sometimes take it off course.

Where can we jump in and help in the search?
Every girl was made uniquely by God, created on purpose for his purpose. Think about the girls you interact with daily. They might have some similarities, but there are also lots of things that set them apart from one another. Each girl is wired with her own specialness, and it's our role as youth workers to help her search and discover the specialness God made.

When I think of this search, I think of Emma. Emma is a leader and a servant. She is generous with her time, she writes thoughtful cards, she never forgets a special occasion, she bakes bread, she is an includer and inviter, she is adventurous, she is REALLY competitive, and she leads a Bible study group of ten middle school girls. She is wired to shepherd middle schoolers. Emma has so many amazing attributes and

Disciplemaking with Girls

characteristics that make her unique. Over time I helped her search for specific ways to put that uniqueness in motion. I watched her discover her spiritual gifts, her heartbeat for youth ministry, and how God wants to use her giftings to impact not only the local church, but her community of unchurched friends from her high school. I don't know another Emma. There is no one like her, and helping her discover that has been one of God's gifts in my own ministry.

Searching for purpose is about so much more than helping girls find a place to use their gifts. It's about discovering and coming to understand our part in God's big story. Discovering our role in building God's kingdom and understanding that he wants to use us to participate in his extraordinary work. We GET to help our girls in this search for purpose and the discovery that follows.

How do we help girls search for their purpose? How do we help girls discover places where they can live out that purpose? We GET to help girls find their purpose in God's purpose for their lives. We GET to point them toward ways to discover their unique story, passions, talents, and spiritual gifts. There is only one of each girl. How do we help them understand how cool that really is? This is one of the key questions we as youth workers need to continually ask ourselves as we minister to teen girls.

SEARCHING FOR TRUTH

Picture this: eight girls and two Bible study leaders sitting in a circle talking about Jesus. The passage being discussed is John 14:6. One of the girls, Victoria, asks a series of rapid-fire questions starting with, "It says Jesus is the truth. How do we know that is true?" Then, "Also, how do we know the Bible is true?" Which leads to, "And how do I know being a Christian is the way to truth? What about my friend who is a Mormon?" Lastly, "How do I know Mormonism *isn't* true?"

It's a little quiet and then I respond, "Okay, cool, Victoria, thank you for that series of really great questions one right after another. I love where your head is at." I look around the group and ask if anyone else has similar questions and nine hands shoot up (my group coleader also has her hand raised—but that's another chapter). Their faces display

Girl World Part 2: The Search

earnest expressions eager and somewhat desperate to know these answers with confidence.

With twenty minutes left on the clock, I look at the group and I say, "Why don't we take one of these questions every week and we will pursue the truth together?"

Truth can be a tricky word these days, since we don't always know how any given human will define it. Today, the journey doesn't seem so focused on *the truth* as it is on "finding my truth" or looking for "truth" that everyone agrees with. Moral relativism and ethical moral relativism often take center stage in our culture, with everyone working to fit truth into their own framework and personal perspective. Barna research shows the progression of this thinking in the book *Gen Z: Vol. 2*:

> Research from 2016 brought to light the prevalence of moral relativism among Gen Z: At a higher proportion than any other generation before them, nearly one in four (24%) strongly agreed that what is morally right and wrong changes over time based on society. Just four years later, that percentage has increased significantly. Nearly one-third (31%) strongly agrees that morality changes in response to social circumstances. Furthermore, another 43 percent agrees somewhat, leaving only one-quarter (26%) who express disagreement (just 10 percent disagree strongly). Moral relativism hasn't just crept into the worldview of Gen Z; it is now the majority opinion. Furthermore, just one-third (34%) strongly affirmed in 2016 that lying is morally wrong (vs. 42% Millennials, 50% Gen X, 54% Boomers, 61% of Elders). There is clear change in the collective moral compass of each successive generation. And as moral relativism grows, universalistic beliefs are increasing in similar fashion: In 2020, two-thirds of teens and young adults (65%) agree that many religions can lead to eternal life, compared with 58 percent in 2016.[3]

In light of this, are teenage girls really searching for *the truth*? Honestly, yes. I have worked with thousands of teenage girls over the years, and almost all of them go down the same line of questioning as Victoria. I don't believe the pursuit for *the truth* has died down. Girls are seeking and searching and looking to discover the truth, and this journey is crucial for every girl. The truth informs so many important things: our moral compass, the way we make decisions, how we relate to others, and our worldview, just to name a few. When we discover *the truth*, it fuels our belief, and belief fuels our confidence as Christ-followers. I believe it's that confidence and assuredness in belief that teenage girls are looking to find.

Where can we jump in and help in the search?
Going back to Victoria's series of questions, I find myself chuckling and shouting YES at the same time. Chuckling because it is just like a ninth grader to pepper you with questions, wanting you to simply and cleanly answer every one before Mom comes to pick up. And shouting YES because, yes yes yes, ask all of the questions to seek *the truth*, Victoria! As we disciple girls in the way of Jesus, we get to help them discover the truth that can only be found in him. We get to create safe spaces for girls to doubt and question and seek answers. Deconstructing the world's view on truth and constructing a perspective built on Jesus. Not being afraid to point them to Matthew 7:7 (NLT) over and over again: "Keep on asking, and you will receive what you ask for. Keep on seeking, and you will find. Keep on knocking, and the door will be opened to you."

We can point girls to Jesus and show them how to ask him questions and listen for responses. We can journey with them through God's Word, helping them discover ways to use it to understand his truth. We GET to be a part of this search for truth, understanding that if girls earnestly search for the truth found in Jesus, they will find it.

SEARCHING TO DO SOMETHING THAT MATTERS IN THE WORLD
The search is on for significance and specialness and making a meaningful impact. Wanting to do something that matters is a marker of today's youngest generations of girls. They are charging after significance with a force unlike that of previous generations. They desire to make a difference in the world and do not want to wait until they are older to do it. With the digital world making the globe seem small, the pandemic, and the growing awareness of social justice, girls

Girl World Part 2: The Search

are searching for ways to do things that impact the greater world, and they fully believe they can.

Where can we jump in and help in the search?
Years ago, I was in a meeting with a pastor from our church and a few of our high school students. We were seeking permission to travel to Rwanda to partner with some churches there. We had built some relationships with a few Rwandan pastors, and we wanted to go and participate in their local community mission work. The pastor told my high school students that it would be very expensive, and did we think we could really accomplish that much in one trip?

Before I could respond, one of the girls in our group, Lauren, spoke up. She shared that we weren't going to solve problems, we were going to encourage, support, and participate in a few specific projects with our partner churches. I smiled and let her continue. She talked about how important partnerships are when it comes to the church. She also said the team would figure out a way to raise the money (our church doesn't allow fundraisers, so this was an interesting thing to toss in). I didn't say five words in this meeting; Lauren's passion far outweighed my leadership. She shared her heart and made a very compelling case, and the pastor eventually approved the trip. Still, I got the impression he remained skeptical and was "humoring the kids," so to speak.

I don't think either of us expected what happened next with this team of students. In the months to follow, they prepped the necessary projects and raised $3,000—on top of their personal trip cost—to assist with two clean water projects. Their commitment, their belief, their creativity, and their passion to minister to the local church in Rwanda went above and beyond what anyone thought they were capable of. They were searching for ways to impact a community for the kingdom of God, and they found them.

I don't share this story to pat these students on the back or to throw one of our pastors under the bus. I share it to illustrate what teens' search for purpose can lead to and what girls are capable of with our partnership. The story of a trip to Africa is unique, but the heart and attitude of Lauren and her team translate to any number of things girls want to go after today.

Disciplemaking with Girls

It is easy for adults to underestimate teenagers or to believe it's best for them to put off this search until they're older, but I think that's a mistake. We GET to be a part of this search for significance. If girls want to change the world, let's encourage the heck out of them. If girls want to innovate new ways to serve God's people, let's get out of the way. If girls want to share the gospel in a remote village in Peru, let's point them in the right direction (literally, we should offer directional help). Imagine what could be possible when the desire to do things that matter and the Holy Spirit partner up inside the hearts of teenage girls. I honestly get goosebumps thinking about this. Lean into this search, people. This is cool.

SEARCHING FOR PEOPLE

Have you ever watched a teenage girl walk into a space where they know no one? I have seen this girl come into my youth ministry countless times. She slowly walks in, takes in the room, and looks around for someone she knows. Whether she is an introvert or an extrovert, there tends to be an initial awkwardness. If she connects with someone in the room, you can physically see the relief wash over her face. If she doesn't find someone, well, a lot of other emotions wash over her face: sadness, fear, tension, or maybe she'll just bury her face in her phone. The desire to be connected to people is a gift that God gave us. He wired us for connection and relationships with others. So, it makes sense that we constantly search for strong connections with other humans. We're searching to discover who knows me, who cares about me, and who are my people? And teen girls are not just searching for *any* people, they are searching for *their people*. Their village. The ones who make them feel known, loved, seen, and cared for. The ones who show up. The ones who text (Maybe call? I am kind of waiting for that to come back into style). The ones who invite and pursue. And they aren't just searching for peers, they're also looking for adults.

According to Barna's research, 45% of Gen Z says that when they feel lonely or anxious, talking to someone other than family helps bring relief.[4] That's not to say that family is not important, it's simply saying that girls value having multiple voices of influence.

We will unpack this more in a later chapter of the book, but I do feel like this search for people is important to mention here too.

Girl World Part 2: The Search

Where can we jump in and help in the search?
Every girl is looking for people. Hopefully, we get to BE those people, but we also get to help them find authentic connections with other believers. What does it look like to help every girl build an Acts 2 community? Read the passage and think about how this might translate to your ministry:

> The Fellowship of the Believers
>
> They devoted themselves to the apostles' teaching and to fellowship, to the breaking of bread and to prayer. Everyone was filled with awe at the many wonders and signs performed by the apostles. All the believers were together and had everything in common. They sold property and possessions to give to anyone who had need. Every day they continued to meet together in the temple courts. They broke bread in their homes and ate together with glad and sincere hearts, praising God and enjoying the favor of all the people. And the Lord added to their number daily those who were being saved.
> — Acts 2:42-47 (NIV)

I love the picture this passage paints of authentic fellowship. It doesn't specify an age range or details about the believers, it simply says "the fellowship of believers." I imagine young and old, men and women, teenagers and kids coming together, eating together, encouraging one another, being generous with what they have, and worshipping God. This is what we should be helping girls seek out—adults and peers who encourage them, lift them in prayer, and worship together weekly, shoulder to shoulder, whether that's in a small group, at Sunday worship service, a midweek Bible study, a Wednesday night youth group, or a living room or coffee shop in the community. We GET to help each girl search for her people. We GET to be part of the village that points her to Jesus every day.

LAST WORDS
When I lose my keys, I am always so grateful for the person in my house who jumps in to help me look. Someone who asks questions, searches with me, and celebrates with me when I find them. That is the

Disciplemaking with Girls

role we can play for teenage girls. We get to jump in and search with them. We can ask questions, retrace steps and learnings, point them to Scripture, and ultimately help them find what they are searching for.

Chapter Four:
Girl World Part 3: Random Axioms

The following are random cool things to know about teenage girls, in no particular order.

GIRLS ARE ATTRACTED TO AUTHENTICITY

In world where many things are not as they seem, girls are looking for real relationships with real people. Leaders who are willing to be transparent and genuine. Leaders who say, "I don't know." Leaders who struggle. Leaders who themselves are on the journey to Jesus. Girls are not attracted to people who appear to have it all together. Girls expect us to meet them right where they are, and they are looking to meet others in that same place.

What does this mean to a youth worker?

- When you ask for a girl's prayer request, be willing to be vulnerable and share your own.
- When you lead and teach, don't only share your hero stories, share the struggles and failures too.
- Examine your heart and your ministry and look for ways to be more transparent.
- Show girls the same person in your social media posts as you are in person.
- Say "I don't know" often. It shows that you are still learning, growing, and curious.

GIRLS ARE NATURALLY EGOCENTRIC

Here's the definition of egocentric: *thinking only of oneself, without regard for the feelings or desires of others; self-centered.*[5]

Disciplemaking with Girls

Ooof. Calling girls egocentric seems kind of savage. But let's be real. It's okay to name this very normal thing about teenage girls. Being egocentric is not their identity, but it is one of the words that describe them at this stage. Most girls exist in a "me" bubble, but I don't believe it's where they desire to live forever. Honestly, when you look back at everything we just talked about—survival, development, searching, and discovering—do you blame them? It's kind of hard not to think of yourself all the time when you are fighting for your life out there (to put it dramatically). There is cause for concern if they never grow out of it, but otherwise we can view girls' self-centeredness as an opportunity to point them outward toward loving God and loving others.

What does this mean to a youth worker?
- Try not to course correct at every self-centered moment. Sometimes you just need to let girls be all about self.
- Look for opportunities to lovingly course correct. I know I just said don't do it…but what I mean is, don't do it *every time*. Look for places to love and guide toward being others-centered.
- Don't mistake ego for identity.
- Serve together. It's hard to think about yourself when you are looking in the eyes of a two-year-old in a church Sunday school class.

GIRLS NEED CONSISTENT ENCOURAGEMENT AND REASSURANCE

There is no such thing as too much encouragement or reassurance for a teenage girl (or for any human, for that matter). This is why we sometimes miscategorize girls as being "needy." I have a love/hate relationship with the word "needy," but sometimes it's the right one to use. Girls are needy for ongoing encouragement and reassurance. This is not a negative. They literally need people from all corners of their lives to build them up through words and actions, affirming their character, choices, achievements, and failures (believe it or not you really can affirm during a failure—it's what helps a girl get back up). Encourage. Reassure. Affirm. Repeat, as often as you can.

What does this mean to a youth worker?
- Send an encouraging text on meaningful days: big math test, an

Girl World Part 3: Random Axioms

audition, an important conversation, opening night.
- Try to leave each conversation with a closing encouraging thought.
- Encourage big and small things. They all matter deeply in the mind of a teenage girl.
- Reassure them often of their relationship with God, the promises of God, how God sees them, prayers from Scripture, and what God calls them to.
- Follow up. Nothing is more encouraging than someone remembering what is going on in your life. Set a billion reminders on your phone and follow up on prayer requests and stories shared.

GIRLS ARE SOCIALLY AWARE

Girls today have a larger awareness of the world than previous generations did. Social media has made the world smaller and more accessible. Girls now have a greater awareness of social justice and a genuine desire to participate or play a part in the stories they see unfolding on a broader scale. They are exposed daily to stories of God's people, points of view, and trends. You might see them donating to someone's GoFundMe to help a dream come true or writing a letter to their local congressperson (or DMing them) to advocate for a particular point of view. Today's younger generations of girls desire to make a difference in this world.

What does this mean to a youth worker?
- Connect the dots between a social issue and how a girl can participate as a Christ-follower.
- Point to prayer, generosity, and sacrifice when a girl wants to engage.
- Listen. If a girl is passionate about something, be a safe place where her voice can be heard.
- It's okay to disagree. You and the girls you work with might not see eye to eye on something. This means you get to practice disagreeing and still loving each other as brothers and sisters in Christ.
- Ask yourself how you can inspire a girl to take the gospel into any of the spaces where she finds herself, online or in person.

Disciplemaking with Girls

GIRLS ARE EASILY INFLUENCED
It's no wonder influencer marketing is super successful with younger generations. Sure, social media posts are carefully curated and timed, but there is a little more to it than that. Girls follow and listen to people they look up to and feel like they relate to, not just in the digital world, but in every space they occupy. Worldview, perspective, faith, attitude, likes, dislikes, and feelings are all easily influenced by the different voices in a girl's day-to-day life. This is not to say that girls are gullible, falling prey to all influences. A girl might have a few people in her life she deems "influential" based on how she perceives them or how she can relate to them. And those influencers are sometimes powerful enough to affect the trajectory of a girl's path.

What does this mean to a youth worker?
- Help girls understand discernment.
- If they are going to find an "influencer" to follow, it might as well be Jesus. How do we point them to the influence of Jesus?
- How do we steward our influence well?
- If a girl has negative influences or influencers in her life, how do we navigate it with her vs. just coming out and telling her "that's wrong" or "that's bad" or "don't do that"? How can we sit in this tension?

GIRLS ARE SENSITIVE, BUT NOT FRAGILE
Teenagers are a little sensitive and rightly so—remember our development convo? But teenage girls do have a sensitivity about them that goes beyond anything I have seen in the guys in my ministry. Girls are sensitive to situations, interactions in relationships, surroundings, and the world's perception of them. Sometimes their sensitivity can be mistaken for fragility. I've always felt there was an unspoken "handle with care" when it comes to girls, implying that we need to tiptoe around them. But being sensitive does not mean you are fragile. Being sensitive is a strength, not a weakness. Sure, there are moments when a girl can be *too* sensitive, but most of the time her sensitivity is picking up something worth looking at more—feelings or emotions or something she has a "sense" about. Sensitivity gives an entry point to understanding and empathy. When we notice what our girls are sensitive to, it helps us pinpoint where to encourage, guide, or reassure them.

Girl World Part 3: Random Axioms

What does this mean to a youth worker?
- If a girl is sensitive to something, take the time to find out her story. Why does she feel the way she does?
- Listen. Repeat. A girl might be sensitive around the same topic and might seem to dwell on something for a long time, over and over again. Show up as many times as you need to.
- Don't shy away from engaging in sensitive conversations. You don't need to have all of the answers.
- Sometimes, it's better not to say anything at all. Presence matters so much.

GIRLS NEED SAFE SPACES
Girls are looking for safe spaces. They need an environment where they can say anything, ask questions without judgment, and be fully themselves. In today's world there are very few places where girls can be vulnerable and trust that they will be heard without condemnation. What if we could give our girls more spaces where they feel completely safe and at ease? I picture a girl walking into a room. Her shoulders rise with an intake of breath, and then they fall with a deep exhale. She is safe here. That is the space a girl needs, a place where she knows she's okay to be fully herself.

What does this mean to a youth worker?
- Examine ministry environments. Is there a way we can make our physical ministry spaces safer and more inviting?
- How can we train other leaders to create safe spaces?
- Consistency builds trust. Showing a girl that you can listen and be discreet will contribute to a safe space.
- A safe space does not mean we do not report or seek help when needed. Some things girls share require us to take action. We need to be intentional about how we hold a girl's trust **and** get her help or involve other adults (parents, therapists, etc.) when needed.

GIRLS HAVE AN AWARENESS OF MENTAL HEALTH
Younger generations are normalizing conversations around mental health. While this can be a taboo topic with stigma attached for older generations, teenagers today are talking about mental health, working

Disciplemaking with Girls

to grow in their awareness of it, and looking for tools to help them navigate it. But although teenagers are "leading up" when it comes to this topic, that doesn't mean they don't need older adults to engage with them.

A recent study by the World Health Organization in November 2021 gives us a snapshot of the current reality:

> Globally, it is estimated that 1 in 7 (14%) 10-19-year-olds experience mental health conditions, yet these remain largely unrecognized and untreated.

- Globally, one in seven 10-19-year-olds experiences a mental disorder, accounting for 13% of the global burden of disease in this age group.
- Depression, anxiety and behavioural disorders are among the leading causes of illness and disability among adolescents.
- Suicide is the fourth leading cause of death among 15-19-year-olds.
- The consequences of failing to address adolescent mental health conditions extend to adulthood, impairing both physical and mental health and limiting opportunities to lead fulfilling lives as adults.[6]

The current percentage of girls struggling with mental health does not seem to be decreasing. Numbers skyrocketed during the pandemic. I can't think of a better place to engage as the church and offer relational discipleship.

What does this mean to a youth worker?
- Learn. I don't think we need to become experts in mental health—those already exist. However, learning basics of mental health, needs/struggles, and tools to address mental health issues can help us to be more effective as ministers.
- Create a resource bank for referrals. What does the church have to offer, what counselors in the community specialize in teenagers,

Girl World Part 3: Random Axioms

and what resources do we or could we keep on hand for girls and parents?
- Understand your role. Only professionals should do the professional work. As youth workers, our role is not to fix or solve problems or give professional advice. Our role is to be *WITH*. To walk with a girl and point her to Jesus, then give guidance toward professional help.
- Show girls practices of rest, sabbath, prayer, singing, and spiritual retreat to create opportunities for connection between God and our mental health.

LAST THOUGHTS

Well, that was a lot. This feels like a good spot for a deep breath.

Why don't you do that. Take a deep breath and then keep reading. Girl world is not for the faint of heart. But I hope you now feel just a little more capable of navigating its crazy terrain. I also hope you picked up important nuggets along the way and grew in your general awareness of teenage girls and how you can enter into their world. The more we seek to understand them, the better leaders we can be.

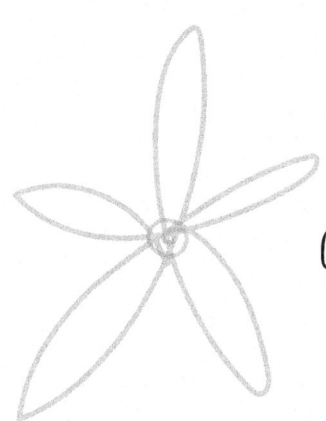

Chapter Five: Perfect Timing

I love perfect timing. When something arrives from Amazon just when you need it, or when someone shows up to help at just the right moment. When cookies come out of the oven perfectly baked, or a check comes in the mail just when a bill is due. When a gas station appears just as the indicator for low fuel illuminates on your dashboard, or your food arrives at the table just as you return from the bathroom.

When I think of teenage girls becoming disciples of Jesus, I can't help but believe that adolescence is the perfect time for a best outcome to begin. I am not saying that this is the *only time* in life that will lead to good outcomes, but simply that the earlier we walk with Jesus, the sooner we live his best life for us.

The teen years are the perfect time for us to offer meaningful, consistent discipleship to our girls.

IT'S THE PERFECT TIME BECAUSE...
GIRLS NEED JESUS.

I know, I know. This is a no-brainer. This idea is the basis of this entire book. But sometimes we need to remind ourselves of the simple things. *Every teenage girl needs Jesus.* Girls need to feel the life-altering love of Jesus. A love that is unconditional and never-ending. Every girl needs to understand that she is not an accident; she was made on purpose for a purpose. Every girl needs to know that Jesus will never leave her. Humans may get it wrong, other people might even abandon her, but he will not. Girls needs to know Jesus will stand strong in her darkest storms and celebrate in her greatest triumphs. Every girl needs to know

Disciplemaking with Girls

Jesus has a best for her. A best life that requires her to leave her old one behind, but will lead to something full and rich. And every girl needs to know life is not easier with Jesus—it's better. Jesus can carry anything she is struggling with. He will not condemn her mistakes, he will forgive her of anything, and he will never roll his eyes at her when she returns to those same behaviors. She needs to know that she belongs to him, and he belongs to her. In a world that is complex and confusing and human and messy, girls need to know Jesus is the way. Gosh, I know that felt a little soap-boxy but man, this the perfect time to disciple teenage girls. They need Jesus so much.

IT'S THE PERFECT TIME BECAUSE...
GIRLS ARE IN THE MOST FORMATIVE YEARS OF THEIR LIVES.

There is no better time than adolescence to begin this process of becoming a disciple of Jesus. Girls in their teenage years are like clay ready to be shaped and molded for God's glory, clay that is transforming and becoming. If girls can know and believe in the importance of being like Christ as teenagers, chances are high they will continue following him in their adult years. And that is the ultimate goal, right? Putting girls on a trajectory toward a *life lived with and for Jesus*.

IT'S THE PERFECT TIME BECAUSE...
THE SEEDS PLANTED WILL EVENTUALLY GROW.

As a leader, I have this ideal in my mind that girls enter the discipleship process in sixth grade eager to grow in a relationship with Jesus and then go off to college after twelfth grade fully devoted and developed disciples. But then I chuckle and come back to reality because the process is rarely that clean and clear.

Discipleship is a "seed-planting" process and the harvest may not happen when I want it to or think it should. I may not even be there when it happens. So, why do it? Well, because seeds play a very significant role in the harvest.

What I am trying to say here is when you ask yourself, "Is anything happening?" or "Is any of this getting through to these girls?" or "Does what I do matter?"—hang in there.

Perfect Timing

Sometimes we as youth workers prepare great sermons, or come up with the perfect illustration, or plan an awesome prayer time... and then we look at the girls in front of us and it seems like no one is paying attention or catching anything we are saying. We look out and see blank faces, ask questions that get no responses, or try to engage in conversation that ultimately feels one-sided.

I once led a Bible study where week after week this one girl—a different girl than the one I mentioned earlier—decided to lie down in our circle about halfway through our discussion. We would be sitting in a circle on the floor, and she would yawn, and then she would straight up just lie down for a good ten minutes. It made me feel so insecure, like I was the worst Bible study leader. But today that girl is a volunteer small group leader at her church and she works at a mission organization focused on helping at-risk youth. If you'd told me this was going to be her story someday when this girl was in junior high, I would have said, "No way. *No way.*" I am actually giggling now thinking about this. God was at work in this girl's life. Seeds were planted and over time those seeds grew into a rich faith.

I have seen this countless times in my ministry to girls. The girl I think isn't paying attention, or is far from Jesus, or has her face buried in her phone, somehow, some way, is still hearing about the things of God.

The disciplemaking process can be slow and there are moments when it seems as if nothing is happening. But faithful and consistent seed-planting eventually yields a harvest.

Conversations, sermons, encouraging texts, camps, car rides, Bible studies, and coffee dates all plant the seeds of Jesus in a girl's heart. None of it is a waste of time. EVERYTHING is an opportunity for a girl to become a stronger disciple of Jesus. God is using every moment and every interaction, even when we can't see it or feel it.

IT'S THE PERFECT TIME BECAUSE...
FAITH PASS-DOWN IS DECREASING.

From the beginning of time, faith has been passed down from generation to generation. Family leadership and discipleship played an important role in each new generation learning to love and live for

Disciplemaking with Girls

Jesus. As time goes on, however, this is lessening. With the percentage of practicing Christians decreasing in the Western world, we will continue to see less family faith pass-down.

Barna's research supports this idea, as seen in this excerpt about the "changing state of the church" in the last twenty years:

> The first and perhaps most significant change we'll explore is that practicing Christians are now a much smaller segment of the entire population. In 2000, 45 percent of all those sampled qualified as practicing Christians. That share has consistently declined over the last 19 years. Now, just one in four Americans (25%) is a practicing Christian. **In essence, the share of practicing Christians has nearly dropped in half since 2000.**
>
> Where did these practicing Christians go? The data indicates that their shift was evenly split. Half of them fell away from consistent faith engagement, essentially becoming non-practicing Christians (2000: 35% vs. 2020: 43%), while the other half moved into the non-Christian segment (2000: 20% vs. 2019: 30%). This shift also contributed to the growth of the atheist / agnostic / none segment, which has nearly doubled in size during this same amount of time (2003: 11% vs. 2018: 21%).[7]

I didn't share this data to freak you out. I am merely suggesting that this is something to pay attention to, for a few reasons. First, in years past, we could expect that parents would bring their kids to our youth ministries. But with fewer parents following Jesus, there could be fewer parents prioritizing having their kids participate in a faith community. We might need to think differently about how we connect teenagers to discipleship. Second, we also might need to adjust our expectations around discipleship happening at home. Some parents might be active in that process, but they also might not be. As youth workers we need to be thoughtful about our partnership with families. And third, we need to be aware that more students might come to us as spiritual blank slates. Girls could show up in our faith communities with no knowledge of the Bible, no faith passed down from parents, and no idea of who Jesus is. This is not scary, this is exciting. If a student comes on their own to explore following Jesus without anyone else's perspective involved, it could lead to a very authentic beginning of a faith in Jesus. But it also means that we can't assume the students we meet have been taught Bible stories since their infancy, or that they've heard the key verses we quote often, or that they know how to pray or read their Bible. A 'blank slate' student is building a faith from scratch.

All of this should motivate us in our disciplemaking. The decrease in faith pass-down means generations of girls are going to need strong followers of Jesus to step up and step in to show them the way. Parents are still the strongest influence in a girl's life, and we should not dismiss or belittle their role. But if parents are not following Jesus, then I suggest that someone will need to share the good news. Who knows, discipling a teenage girl could lead to her whole family knowing Jesus too!

IT'S THE PERFECT TIME BECAUSE… OF WHAT A GIRL COULD BE.

When I first begin discipling a teenage girl, I can't help but think of *what could be*. By nature, I am a 'glass half full' kind of a person. But my sense of *'what could be'* is not tied to my optimism, it's connected to what could be possible if a teenage girl surrenders her heart to Jesus. What could be if God got a hold of her gifts, her passion, her mind, her creativity, and her experiences? How could he use her in the lives of others? How could he use her to write beautiful things that inspire or encourage? How could he use her to build his kingdom and share the gospel with the people in her world? How could he use her to teach others his Word? There are so many possibilities of what God could do with a willing and surrendered heart. The teenage years are the perfect time to disciple a girl simply because there is a powerful sense of possibility—of *what could be*.

Dream with me for a minute. The girls we disciple now are…
- Future members of the workforce
- Future pastors
- Future friends
- Future parents
- Future church leaders

Disciplemaking with Girls

- Future social media influencers
- Future writers, podcasters, and content creators
- Future neighbors
- Future scientists, teachers, doctors, chefs, lab techs, bankers, designers, and the list goes on

A girl who loves Jesus and lives fully for him in all of the spaces she occupies is a powerful force. Think of what could be and allow that to inspire how you engage now.

IT'S THE PERFECT TIME BECAUSE… IF NOT NOW, THEN WHEN?

If not now, when? The life with and for Jesus is right now! The longer a girl walks with Jesus the longer she will live in richness with him. Now is the time for us to be bold and lead and guide and shepherd and put girls on the path to becoming strong disciples of Jesus. Because if not in the most formative years of their lives, then when? When will we have another opportunity like this?

It makes me think about my own journey with Jesus. For most of my teenage years, I was the only Christian in my home. My high school small group leader, Marcy, led me to Christ. Jesus became the Lord of my life when I was fourteen and I have been walking with him ever since. Of course my journey with Jesus has had its ups and downs, but I'm grateful I met him when I did.

My parents did not know Jesus, nor did they take me to church growing up. I was one of those 'blank slates' way back then. If the youth group leaders at the church hadn't shared Jesus with me, taught me about him, and showed me the way to a relationship with him, I wonder where I would be today. I am grateful for Marcy's consistency, her boldness, the fact that she showed up every week, and her willingness to be transparent about her own faith. She taught me to read my Bible and pray and encouraged me weekly in my journey with Jesus. There are things that I learned at fourteen, fifteen, and sixteen that I still practice and that still inspire my faith today. When I look back over the thirty-plus years I have been a follower of Jesus, I feel so grateful I didn't meet him just two years ago. I have had so much of my life with him, and it has been so full and lovely and rich. It has not been without heartache and pain and struggle, but I have always had God's guiding hand in my toughest moments. What a gift. I want every teenage girl to experience that gift. Now is the perfect time to engage because when we do, we give girls the opportunity to maximize a lifetime with Jesus. If not now, then when? And if not us, then who?

LAST THOUGHTS

Hopefully by now the puzzle of teenage girls is taking shape and you are starting to see the 'picture on the box' come together. Believe it or not there are still some pieces I left out. The last few pieces I'll cover will show up with each girl you walk with. The puzzle will continue to take shape as you meet each unique girl in her discipleship process.

Part Two:
WITH IS THE WAY

Disciplemaking with Girls

Just about every person I meet tells me that my daughter Abby is my 'mini me.' We don't look exactly alike, but we have very similar mannerisms, our voice inflections happen in the same places, we have the same sense of humor, we use a lot of the same sayings, and we can apply quotes from *The Office* to any life situation. It makes sense to me when people say, "You and Abby are so much alike." When you spend the kind of time Abby and I have together, resembling one another is only natural. I realize Abby and I are related and that it's especially natural for parents and their kids to look alike or act alike, but I believe any relationship that includes committed time together, consistent proximity, shared experiences, and intentional conversation can end up yielding results like these. One person picks up on the attributes and characteristics of the other and then emulates those characteristics in their own life.

This is just like disciplemaking, where a life for Jesus impacts another life. This is what happens when mature Christ-followers walk with teenage girls on a journey that ultimately has them 'resembling Jesus.' By watching mature Christ-followers in action, girls can develop characteristics that reflect him, a stronger belief in him, values that mirror his, and a heart that lives for him.

For this to happen, girls need a handful of influential people to come alongside them. Not just any people, but people who deeply love Jesus. People in active pursuit of Jesus. People who are a few steps ahead in their own journey with Jesus. And people who lead by example. In the sea of voices in the world, girls need a few influential ones that will loudly point them to Jesus and the life he has for them.

If we want to see girls become strong disciples, they need to see what a life with Jesus looks like through the examples of mature and godly women and men. So we need to ask ourselves: Who are these people, and where do we find them? What characteristics are crucial in someone who is going to disciple teenage girls? As we move into the chapters ahead, we are going to spend some time unpacking the powerful impact of relational discipleship, building a team of disciplemakers, and equipping that team to disciple teenage girls. Because relationships are a key component of disciplemaking, it's worth our time to think about WHO we are asking to be disciplemakers,

WHAT they will do, and HOW they will be the most effective in their role.

Chapter Six:
Relational Discipleship

A few years ago, I was having a conversation with my friend and mentor Rob Jacobs. Rob is someone who thinks deeply about personal discipleship and has a passion to help everyone around him become a stronger disciple of Jesus. He is also one of those annoying people who asks me challenging questions, but never gives me any answers. Do you have those people in your life?

Anyway, we were talking about discipleship in our church, and he asked me what approach we took in our youth ministry to help teenagers becoming stronger disciples of Jesus. I started explaining our programs, events, and all the calendar items to help him understand what our ministry was accomplishing week to week. He looked at me thoughtfully, smiled, and said, "Wow, you have a lot of cool stuff happening in the youth ministry, but that wasn't my question. What is your approach to discipleship? How do you help teenagers know Jesus, follow Jesus, and live for Jesus?"

I sat there for a minute, unsure of how to answer. My mind had gone straight to our youth ministry's strategy and structure and programs, but he wasn't asking about any of that. In his kindness he affirmed everything we were doing, and he wasn't saying that any of it wasn't valuable—he was simply challenging me to think differently about discipleship. Helping me distinguish the difference between a program and something more personal for a teenager.

As we continued to talk, he asked me, "If you could describe your discipleship strategy in one word, what would it be?" I immediately answered, "Relationships." I told him we believe relationships are the

Disciplemaking with Girls

key to helping a teenager follow and walk with Jesus in their daily life. I explained about the importance of mature believers walking with teenagers in relationships. Relationships seemed to be the most effective way to approach discipleship.

Rob went to whiteboard, as he often does, and wrote down the word *RELATIONSHIPS*.
Rob: "I heard you say relationships are the key."
Me: "Yep."

And then he wrote down another word—*WITH*.
Rob: "I also heard you say *with one another*."
Me: "Yes, adults walking with teenagers in their journey with Jesus."

And then he wrote down one last phrase: *WITH is the way*.
Rob: "I have been chewing on this phrase lately."
Me: Speechless for thirty seconds. Then, "Wow, I love that phrase. I love what it represents. I love the picture it paints. Yes. With is the way."

He told me he had been thinking about this phrase when it came to how we approached whole-church discipleship. Something clicked for me in that moment. Rob put simple language around something I was making more complex than it needed to be. When pressed, I boiled discipleship down to the word *relationships*, so why was I usually thinking it needed to be more complex? As I sat there staring at the whiteboard, that phrase began to rattle around in my brain.

With is the way.
Relational discipleship.
With is the way.
Growing to be like Jesus **with** *one another in relationship.*
With *is relational discipleship.*
Relational discipleship is the best way to make disciples.
Something I've always known, but needed language for.
Thank you, Rob.

RELATIONAL DISCIPLESHIP

Relational discipleship is the most effective approach to disciplemaking with teenage girls. A mature disciple of Jesus walking *WITH* a teenage

Relational Discipleship

girl, showing her how to follow Jesus and live for him. A relationship that includes time, consistent proximity, intentional conversation, and shared experiences to help a girl become a stronger disciple of Jesus. There are different ways to approach discipleship and all sorts of approaches to learning. But what it all comes down to is relationships.

To use an analogy, you can learn *about* swimming from a book, but you can't learn *how* to swim from a book. You learn by getting in the pool. When you get in the water, the instructor first *tells* you how to swim, then they *show* you, then they swim *with* you, and then they turn you loose to swim on your own. You can learn about being a disciple of Jesus from books, devotionals, podcasts, YouTube, etc., but nothing will be as impactful as the learning that comes from a relationship with a more mature believer, from someone walking with you and helping you jump into the deep end.

This is how Jesus did it.

When we look at how Jesus made disciples, it is undeniable that relationships are at the center. His model IS relationships. He shaped and formed twelve men by sharing life with them. He walked with them, ate with them, served with them, and prayed with them. The disciples saw him pause on the road to love people well, listened to him teach, and watched him perform countless miracles. It was in their *relationship with* Jesus that they were able to grasp his beliefs, values, heart, and teachings.

Look at this quote from *Mentoring for Mission*. It's kind of an older book on discipleship, but I love how Krallmann encapsulates this concept:

> Through the disciples' continual exposure to who he was, what he did and said, Jesus intended them to discern and absorb his vision, mindset and mode of operation. He desired them to become so saturated with the influences arising from his example and teaching, his attitudes, actions and anointing, that every single area of their lives would be impacted towards greater likeness to himself. The approach he decided on was simple and informal, practical and wholistic. The totality of

shared life experiences made up the disciples' classroom, and their teacher's words merely needed to further elucidate the lessons already gained from his life.[8]

Man, I love the picture this quote paints. Side note: I had to look up the word *elucidate* in the dictionary. If it's helpful, it means *to make things clear* and it's a verb.

Imagine life together with Jesus impacting every corner of the disciples' lives. Doing life so closely that they were *"saturated with the influences arising from his example."* Everything helping them find a greater likeness with Jesus. And Jesus utilizing multiple avenues of learning and life together to bring about that likeness, with an approach that is *"simple and informal, practical and wholistic."* So often we as humans complicate what doesn't need to be complicated. When it comes to disciplemaking we tend to think intricate plans and programs yield the best results. But if we look at the approach of Jesus, we see one powerful tool take center stage: relationships.

Let's take a closer look at Jesus's approach.

Matthew 4:18-19 (NLT)
One day as Jesus was walking along the shore of the Sea of Galilee, he saw two brothers—Simon, also called Peter, and Andrew—throwing a net into the water, for they fished for a living. Jesus called out to them, "Come, follow me, and I will show you how to fish for people!"

Relational discipleship: Jesus invites Simon and Andrew into something *with* him and tells them he will show them what to do! He is not just telling the disciples what to do or what should be done, he is going to *SHOW* them how. Imagine what would have stuck with Peter and Andrew after moments with Jesus where he showed them how to be "fishers of men."

Luke 11:1-4 (NLT)
Once Jesus was in a certain place praying. As he finished, one of his disciples came to him and said, "Lord, teach us to pray, just as John taught his disciples." Jesus said, "This is how you should pray: 'Father, may your name be kept holy. May your Kingdom come soon. Give us

Relational Discipleship

each day the food we need, and forgive us our sins, as we forgive those who sin against us. And don't let us yield to temptation.'"

Relational discipleship: The disciples saw the importance Jesus placed on prayer. They got to watch him take time away to pray often. There are two things I love about this. First, that one of the disciples asked Jesus to teach them how to pray. I love how relationships allow us to be vulnerable and ask for help and instruction when they are needed. Second, Jesus responds immediately with thoughtful instructions on how to pray. He also gives a sample prayer with tangible elements to hang onto to help them pray in the future. This moment shows us the give and take of relational discipleship, the role of the disciple and the role of the disciplemaker.

Matthew 5:1-2 (NLT)
One day as he saw the crowds gathering, Jesus went up on the mountainside and sat down. His disciples gathered around him, and he began to teach them.

Relational discipleship: The disciples were travelling around with Jesus. Think of all the places they gathered around him as he taught the crowds. Think of what took place as they walked from place to place. Imagine the conversations that might have been. And then imagine the actual teaching. Sitting at the feet of Jesus, listening to his every word. I would guess the disciples picked up a lot listening to the teaching, but I also wonder what they observed during the in-between moments of travel with Jesus.

John 13:12-15 (NLT)
After washing their feet, he put on his robe again and sat down and asked, "Do you understand what I was doing? You call me 'Teacher' and 'Lord,' and you are right, because that's what I am. And since I, your Lord and Teacher, have washed your feet, you ought to wash each other's feet. I have given you an example to follow. Do as I have done to you. I tell you the truth, slaves are not greater than their master. Nor is the messenger more important than the one who sends the message. Now that you know these things, God will bless you for doing them."

Disciplemaking with Girls

Relational discipleship: This might be one of the more powerful moments between Jesus and his disciples. Here is another picture of Jesus inviting the disciples into an experience with him. He doesn't just wash their feet, he serves them, he shows great humility, he tells them what it means to serve one another, and he instructs them to follow his example in the future. Again, can you imagine how this moment impacted the disciples? Watching the master wash your feet? Imagine the way a moment like this could encourage or empower or inspire. Wow.

This is the power of relational discipleship.

Jesus knew it.

He modeled it and gave us a picture for how to do it. He showed us the way that would yield the best results.

Life together *with* fellow believers. Life *with* one another. Jesus *taught* them, then *showed* them how, then *invited* them into experiences with him, and then *empowered* them to live it out.

We get to do this with teenage girls.
We get to show the way.
We get to model how.
We get to encourage and empower.
We get to send out.

Think of what is possible for a girl in the context of relationships like that.

Relationships with adults who lead by example, share faith experiences, and do life together. Leaders who emulate Christ and show girls how to do that too.

Leaders who will…
Worship with
Pray with
Serve with
Cry with

Grieve with
Experience with
Grow with
Study with
Walk with
Talk with

It's exciting to think about what God could do in the heart of a teenage girl through this kind of relationship.

LAST THOUGHTS

Relational discipleship isn't new. This is something Jesus put into motion a long time ago. So what would happen if we followed his lead now and lived out what he modeled for us? The power in this process is found in his method.

And doesn't it just feel good and right to follow Jesus's lead?

Chapter Seven:
Building a Team of Disciplemakers

When I look around my church, I see a lot of different teenage girls. No two are alike.

I see Paige. She was invited to church by a friend, and that same friend led her to Jesus at our winter camp. Paige's parents don't know Jesus and have never stepped foot inside our church. Her journey to becoming a stronger disciple is unique.

I see Kate. She loves Jesus deeply. She is actively pursuing her relationship with him and always looking for ways to deepen her connection to him. Kate's dad took his life a few years ago. She lives with an unpredictable grief that is sometimes manageable and sometimes hits like a tidal wave. Her journey to becoming a stronger disciple is unique.

I see Rachel. She is shy and reserved and often stands off to the side of the action. She likes Jesus a lot, but hasn't yet surrendered her heart to him. She is curious and sometimes asks questions I can't answer. She's seeking and questioning and searching. Her journey to becoming a stronger disciple is unique.

I see Shelley. She just came to church for the first time ever a few weeks back. Her eyes are wide, but she came back three weeks in a row. She knows nothing about Jesus. Everything is new. Her journey to becoming a stronger disciple is unique.

Every teenage girl is on her own unique journey with Jesus. This uniqueness requires an equally unique disciplemaker to walk alongside her.

Disciplemaking with Girls

Where do we begin when it comes to building a team of consistent, diverse, spiritually mature leaders to disciple teenage girls? How do we find unique leaders to walk with our unique girls?

Whether you are building a team of leaders to disciple the girls in your youth ministry or building a personal disciplemaking team around one specific teenage girl, you need the right people for the job. Over the next few pages, we'll look at key areas to consider as you build a team of leaders to journey with the girls in your ministry:

- What makes a great leader?
- What are you inviting them to?
- Who are you looking for?
- Where do you find them?

WHAT MAKES A GREAT LEADER?
Years ago, I met with Vivian, a woman from our church who wanted to lead ninth grade girls. The first question I asked was why she wanted to disciple girls. She launched into a thirty-minute narrative about the world and the behavior she was seeing in young girls today. She told me she wanted to "set girls on the narrow path to Jesus." She told me she had so much wisdom to share and so many things to teach. She had written Bible studies that would help girls turn from wickedness, temptation, and sin.

After about an hour together, it was clear to me that she would not be a good fit for the role. Not once did she show any empathy for what girls are going through. She didn't talk about her love for girls or for the age. She didn't mention anything about meeting girls where they are or helping them grow in their relationship with Jesus. She talked about what *she* would do to fix the problems she saw.

Now, she was a lovely woman who loved our church and loved Jesus. And I do believe she had a genuine desire for girls to know Jesus more. But she was not the person I was looking for to be our ninth grade girls small group leader. She viewed girls as a mess she was going to clean up. This was an easy no for me.

Although teenage girls can sometimes be a bit of mess, I am not looking for people to clean up that mess. I am looking for people to *step into* the mess with girls.

When I meet with people who want to disciple teenage girls, I am listening for and looking for a few qualities I believe a leader needs to possess. This woman had a few of them, but not enough to green light her for ministry on our team.

Having a clear picture of who we are looking for helps us find the best people for the role, the ones who are wired to disciple teenage girls. If we don't take the time to carefully look for the right leaders, we could end up with lovely people on our team who end up doing more harm than good.

The following six attributes are good ones to be on the lookout for when building of team of leaders to disciple girls. In your setting or context you might add more specific things.

Loves Jesus
No brainer? Yes. But we should still talk about it. Since Jesus's model revolves around setting an example to follow, it's important to set some standards for spiritual maturity among our leaders. It would be tough to lead a girl on a discipleship journey without being a disciple yourself. Disciples make disciples. Girls need leaders who have a confidence in their belief in and relationship with Jesus. When it comes to building a team of leaders and disciplemakers, establishing a few key expectations for spiritual maturity is important.

Some things to look for:
- Actively pursuing Jesus
- Accountability relationships with other believers
- Participant in the greater church
- Showing the fruit of the Spirit in their life
- Can articulate the gospel and share it with a teenage girl (again, I know this seems like a no brainer, but you should still ask)

I am not suggesting that to serve, people need to check the boxes of a spiritual checklist, but I do think it's worth our time to understand a leader's heart for Jesus and discern if they are in a stage and place to disciple. It's okay to say, "not now" to someone who needs to grow in their own discipleship before they step into a role like this. Of course, every follower of Jesus is on a journey. I am not suggesting the standards need to be crazy high, but I do believe you should *have* standards.

Likes teenage girls

Again, no brainer? Yes. But still an important thing to look for. When I met with Vivian, I never heard her express her love or even her *like* for teenage girls. I don't think you need to look for people who love teenage girls, just for those who really like them a lot. What's the difference? Well, everyone must *love* teenage girls "in the name of Jesus"—but *liking* them is another story. People who *like* teenage girls find humor and joy and delight in being around them. Don't get me wrong, teenage girls can be scary and intimidating, but you are looking for the people who won't be deterred by any stereotypes. They just genuinely enjoy being in their presence.

Some things to listen for when you talk to potential leaders:
"I just love the way they…"
"It cracks me up when girls say…"
"They are so fun to be around…"
"I can't wait to spend time with…"

If a leader likes teenage girls, they will show up consistently and naturally will be more effective in their discipleship role.

Authentic

I mentioned the importance of authenticity in a previous chapter, and it's worth examining again now. Teenage girls value people who are authentic, transparent, and willing to lead in real conversations. When leading young people, it is easy to feel the pressure to have it all together or know all the answers. But girls are not looking for a perfect leader who knows everything. They are looking for someone to show up and say, "I am in it with you." Leaders who know how to be themselves, leaders who can say, "I don't know," and leaders who are willing to share their journey with girls.

Some things to look for:
- Humility
- Teachable/coachable
- Willing to say, "I don't know"

Authenticity in a leader shows girls that we are all on a lifelong journey to becoming stronger disciples. At the same time, girls value having someone a little further ahead in the process to show them the way.

Committed to consistency

One of the things I love about the teacher/student relationship is the consistency and the opportunities that consistency presents. Those relationships end up being some of the most influential ones in kids' lives. Why? Well, think about the impact of a student spending consistent time every week with the same adult at the same time (for the most part) for eight months out of the year. Time plus relationship opens doors for influence and impact. The same is true in the discipleship process with teenage girls. Having an adult or adults who show up consistently can lead to significant impact and influence. Girls need leaders who have the time to be consistent. Leaders who are present on a regular basis will be able to journey with girls in daily life.

Some things to look for:
- A schedule that has time; not overcommitted
- An understanding of the importance of consistency with girls

It doesn't matter if it's quantity time or quality time or formal time or casual time. What matters is that time is spent together consistently. The real impact is in the consistency.

Encouraging

We live in a world that seems to thrive on negativity, and we need to surround girls with leaders conveying another message. Every facet of the discipleship process requires encouragement. Encouraging a girl to go to Jesus with her struggle. Encouraging a girl to understand who God made her to be. Offering encouraging words that are loving and kind and uplift a girl's spirit. Encouraging a girl with one of the

Disciplemaking with Girls

God's promises during a tough moment. Encouraging a girl to mend a friendship within a small group. Encouraging a girl to share her story with someone who doesn't know Jesus. When you think about it, discipleship and encouragement are somewhat synonymous. Girls need leaders who are intentional about their encouragement.

When you talk with a potential leader, ask how they would encourage a teenage girl. If you do not sense a general excitement around encouragement in their response, then it's best for you to tell them no thank you. Nicely, of course.

Lights up

I was working at a coffee shop the other day when a pack of teenage girls walked in. There were about nine of them and they were loud and excited. I think they were already highly caffeinated, but here they were, ready to load back up with sugar and caffeine. I happened to glance over at the barista behind the counter when the girls walked in and I saw the biggest eye roll of all time. I couldn't tell if she was annoyed or defeated or scared, but she had a look. I think the look was connected to the fact that she was about to be asked to make nine Frappuccinos from the secret menu. Poor girl.

This moment illustrated the way most people receive teenage girls. How would the exchange between the barista and the girls be different if the barista was super excited to see them? What if she was overjoyed that they walked into her coffee shop?

Girls need leaders who are the people in the room the most excited to see them. Leaders who communicate value and care by the way they light up with delight to be in teen girls' presence. Leaders who can't wait for the pack of teenage girls to walk through the door so that they can receive them with warmth and joy and the love of Jesus. It's the light of a leader that draws a girl into the light of Jesus.

WHAT ARE YOU INVITING POTENTIAL LEADERS TO?

One Sunday morning, I stood in front of our church and talked about our need for volunteers to come and disciple teenagers in weekly small groups. I talked about what a great opportunity it was for God to use them, how fun it was to work with teenagers, and how big the need

Building a Team of Disciplemakers

was. After the service was over, a woman walked up to me and said she was interested in serving, but she had one question. She asked, "can you explain what the need actually is?" I thought to myself, *Oh yeah, I didn't talk about what I was inviting them into.* I simply said "come work with teenagers in our youth ministry, it will be really fun."

This got me thinking about how I communicate the invitation into relational discipleship. What are the important things someone would need to know before saying yes to that ask?

When we invite leaders to play a role in discipleship, it's wise to think about our invitation. What needs to be shared with a potential leader to give them a glimpse of the role we want them to play? There are three key areas we can share to help potential leaders understand what we are inviting them into. First, the vision. Next, the commitment and leadership expectations. Lastly, the process for joining the team. Let's drill down into these three areas.

Share the WHY

A great place to start with potential leaders is **the why behind discipleship.** Take time to share the vision around the role you want them to play. This does not need to be complicated; it could be as simple as a few sentences helping a potential leader grasp the heart for the ministry and goal for their role.

Questions that help form **the why:**
- What is the desired end result for every girl?
- Why does this program/event/small group exist?
- What is the need?
- Is there a problem that needs to be solved?
- What do you hope every girl/leader experiences?
- Where and when does discipleship happen?

Below is a sample of a vision sheet I have given small group leaders in the past. The goal of this document is to give a potential leader a glimpse of what I am inviting them into. It's simple, meant to operate as a springboard into conversation.

Vision Sheet for Small Group Leaders

THE NEED
There are thousands of teenage girls living in our immediate community who need to know the transforming love of Jesus Christ. Girls are in need of godly men and women to come alongside them and help them know Jesus, love Jesus, and ultimately become like Jesus.

THE VISION
To help teenage girls become stronger disciples of Jesus Christ

HOW WE FULFILL THE VISION
We help teenage girls become like Jesus through relationships (with godly adults and peers), fun, teaching w/an emphasis on biblical literacy, faith-building experiences, and participation in the church body.

THE HOPE FOR EVERY GIRL
- We **hope** every girl understands the gospel and the way it transforms her life.
- We **hope** every girl grows in her love for Jesus.
- We **hope** every girl grows in her knowledge of God's Word.
- We **hope** every girl connects with a godly woman in a discipleship relationship.
- We **hope** every girl lives life with and for Jesus.
- We **hope** every girl understands she was made on purpose for God's purpose.

THE VIBE* WE VALUE
*****The vibe sets the stage for discipleship to happen**
- Centered on Jesus
- Relational
- Thoughtful about who's in the room
- Warm environments
- Safe spaces for authenticity
- Laughter, humor, lightheardness, fun

THE PLACES WHERE WE FULFILL THE VISION
- Small groups (gender & age specific)
- Sunday church service (same times as adult sunday services)[9]

As you can see, the sample I provided is not a robust description of everything a leader does in their discipleship role, but it is a glimpse to give an idea of what is ahead. Taking time to shape and share **the why** before people join the team helps make the invitation a little more attractive.

Share the commitment and the expectations of the role

We are inviting potential leaders into a life-on-life ministry role. The kind of role that requires time, consistency, and some leadership skills. It's important that we communicate the time commitment and expectations around the role to help a potential leader understand what they are saying yes to.

Questions that shape **commitment level and expectations:**

- What kind of time commitment is required? (time frames, frequency)
- What roles do you expect leaders to play?
- What is the discipleship journey for a leader and a girl?
- How will you know discipleship with teenage girls is successful?
- What is my dream for discipleship? (Sometimes this question helps potential leaders jump outside the box and work new, innovative elements into a ministry plan)

The following is a sample of what I share with a potential leader when asking them to think about joining our team to disciple teenage girls. We'll look at this even more in an upcoming chapter. For context, small groups are not the only avenue for discipleship in our ministry, but they are a primary space where it happens.

Small Group Leader Role

THINGS TO DO ONCE A WEEK (3-4 hours)

- ☐ Pray for each girl in your group.
- ☐ Prepare for leading/teaching your small group (2 hours).
- ☐ Show up to your small group each week.
- ☐ Lead/teach your small group.
- ☐ Send a personal text to each girl.
- ☐ Follow up on any care or questions.

THINGS TO DO ONCE A MONTH (4-6 hours)

- ☐ Connect with three girls outside of your typical small group time.
- ☐ Plan something that builds relationships or a faith-building experience.
- ☐ Send a parent email sharing about your group.

THINGS TO DO EACH SEMESTER

- ☐ Strive to have one significant conversation with every girl in your group.
- ☐ Connect with other small group leaders for prayer and encouragement.
- ☐ Create a calendar for the girls and parents (include content, fun, and opportunities to serve).[10]

Building a Team of Disciplemakers

It's important to give some details to help a leader decide if they can commit to relational discipleship. Sharing **the commitment and expectations** before people join the team helps make the invitation a little more attractive.

Share the process

We've talked about the *why* and the *what*, so now let's talk about the *how*. When you give an invitation to a potential leader, it's wise to share the process for joining the team. Again, it doesn't need to be complicated, nor does it need be a twenty-five-point process, but it should be enough to give you the opportunity to assess if someone is a fit for the role of leading teenage girls. I was grateful to have a process in place when I met with Vivian. She wasn't a fit for the role, and the process gave us the time, space, and information to make that call.

Questions that shape **the process** for becoming a leader:
- What steps do leaders need to take to join the team?
- Does my church or organization require anything specific for leaders working with teenagers?
- What are good questions to ask to gain a deeper understanding of someone's heart, character, and relationship with Jesus?
- What are good questions to ask that help assess availability, fit, and background?
- What information do I need to collect?

Below is a sample of the process I invite potential leaders to go through before determining whether they're a fit for discipling teenage girls. This is the journey Vivian and I went on together. (We made it to step 4.)

Disciplemaking with Girls

> **Process for Potential Leaders**
>
> **STEP 1:** Initial invite conversation
>
> **STEP 2:** Fill out an application
>
> **STEP 3:** Background check, reference check
>
> **STEP 4:** Interview/assess fit
>
> **STEP 5:** Orientation
>
> **STEP 6:** Training/equipping for discipleship role
>
> **STEP 7:** Connect and begin discipling students[11]

A simple process like this can give you and the potential leader time to discern if this is the role for them. Discipling teenage girls is important. It's a big commitment and the leader will be highly influential in teens' lives. Having steps like these in place helps ensure that we connect the very best people to our girls. Taking time to shape and share **the how** before people join the team helps make the invitation a little more attractive.

WHO ARE WE LOOKING FOR?

Linda is a new leader on our team this year. She just stepped up to disciple and lead a group of freshman girls. Her personality is a little reserved. She is a former third grade teacher, and she has never led a small group before. Oh, and did I mention she is in her seventies? On paper, Linda doesn't necessarily scream "high school girls discipleship." She's not the twenty-something influencer type we might imagine for this role. But when you meet Linda, you quickly understand that she is consistent, kind, faithful, creative, and bakes the best desserts. She has been walking with Jesus for most of her life and is a deep well of knowledge and wisdom. She is honest and kind and isn't afraid of any conversation topic. She is a gift to the girls she is discipling this year.

I am telling you about Linda because it can be easy to believe certain types of leaders are the best disciplemakers for teen girls, maybe someone young, cool, and extroverted, with loads of free time and an

SUV. But the truth is girls come in all shapes and sizes; therefore we need to look for disciplemakers of all shapes and sizes. We need to shatter any stereotypes we might have because every person has the potential to connect with a teenage girl and point her toward becoming like Jesus.

With all of that in mind, what should we keep in mind as we search for who to invite to the team?

Girls need women

Girls need women to disciple them. The end. Just kidding, there's more—but that really is the most important thing to grasp. Every girl needs at least one or two women walking closely with her in her journey. Women other than Mom or an immediate family member who are committed to helping a teenage girl become like Jesus. Don't get me wrong, there is a place for parents/guardians/immediate family and other people in a girl's life. We will talk about them in a minute. But teenage girls specifically need to rub shoulders with women who love Jesus. They need to see women following Jesus. They need to serve alongside women serving Jesus. They need to hear women teaching and glean from their perspective. They need to see women leading and pastoring and kingdom-building. They need to see women pursuing Jesus in their daily lives. They need to see women struggle and doubt and ask big questions. Girls need godly women modeling a life lived with and for Jesus. There are things that only women can model to teenage girls.

- No one can empathize with teenage girls like women.
- No one can give unique faith footsteps to follow like women.
- No one can talk about women in Scripture, women in the church, and women in ministry like women.
- No one can give vision for future roles girls might play in God's work like women.

Bottom line: teenage girls need women investing in them weekly and pointing the way to Jesus. When you think about who you are going to invite to the team, make it a priority to invite women who love Jesus deeply and like teenage girls a lot.

Disciplemaking with Girls

Girls need more than one
One discipleship relationship is great, but a few is better. I am not sure if there is a magic number here, but I do know it's a really good thing to have multiple people walk alongside of a girl. Not everyone needs to engage in the discipleship process in the same capacity, but they should all be consistent and keep in mind the goal of the relationship—to help girls in their journey with Jesus.

Some of the different leader roles that strengthen a disciple:
- Prayer warrior
- Ministry leader/supervisor
- Youth pastor
- Vocational ministry mentor
- Encourager

When you think about who you are going to invite to disciple teenage girls, think bigger than just one leader per girl. Think about leaders with different gifts, capacities, and roles who could potentially help a teenage girl become a stronger disciple of Jesus.

Girls need men
I often get asked if men can play a role in discipling teenage girls. The answer is YES. I understand why this question gets asked, but it is crucial for men to be investing in young women. Men and women were made in the image of God to be in partnership with one another. I believe the discipleship of teenage girls is a very powerful place for that partnership to play out. Just as girls need to watch women follow Jesus, they also need to see men following Jesus. Discipleship relationships with men will look different than the relationships with women, but they still offer meaningful guidance and encouragement in a girl's journey with Jesus. I recommend putting in place and enforcing thoughtful boundaries when it comes to the relationships between men and teenage girls. Promoting healthy and safe relationships should be a top priority and is a no-brainer. Whether it's teaching a sermon or an encouraging conversation or leading in a faith experience, there are a number of ways men can help strengthen a female disciple.

Girls need diversity

Remember Linda? She's our reminder to shatter any stereotype we have regarding what makes a great leader. Teenage girls need leaders of all ages, backgrounds, ethnicities, and preferences. Since no two teenage girls are alike, we should see diversity across our leadership teams. We want to make sure our leaders represent 'who is in the room' among our teenage girls. All girls do not like the same stuff, dress alike, or come from the same background. Building a team with this in mind helps us foster more meaningful connections with girls.

WHERE DO WE FIND LEADERS?

Gosh, this is the million-dollar question, right? Where do we find leaders to disciple teenage girls? At times this search feels impossible, especially given that everyone in the church is competing for the same pool of people, the overall busyness of our culture, and the stereotypes we are trying to bust about teenagers.

My greatest ongoing need as a youth pastor is more leaders. How to find more leaders might be the number one question I get asked by other youth workers. Where do we find leaders to disciple teenage girls? Honestly, if I could answer this with 100% certainty, I could have charged double for this book. JK. But really, it is a big question that every team-builder is looking to answer.

I might not have all the answers, but I do know where I have seen success within my own youth ministry. The following is a list of ideas that will hopefully spark more creative, wonderful, and innovative ideas from you.

Begin with prayer

It can be easy to overlook this step, but resist the temptation to jump ahead. Take the time to bring your needs, your wants and everything else to Jesus before you start looking for people. Get into a mindset and posture of following his lead when it comes to building your team of disciplemakers.

Seriously: This is important.

Disciplemaking with GIRLS

Ask the girls
This is one of the best places to find leaders. Talk to the girls those leaders will be working with. Who do your girls look up to? Whose faith do they want to emulate? They have an inside track to people you don't. Teachers, coaches, other kids' parents they think are cool, and other people from spaces you don't occupy. Once you ask them for ideas, send your girls out to "make the ask." It is hard to turn down a girl asking you to disciple her.

Rely on current people
This is by far where I have found the most success. The most powerful testimony is that of a satisfied customer. A current leader who loves their role can be a great inviter of new leaders. Also, everything is more fun with a friend. Leading teenage girls is less intimidating and more fulfilling when you get to do it with someone you know. Asking current leaders to recruit their best friend, or a friend who is the best fit, just might double your team overnight!

Look in unexpected places
Everyone you meet is a potential leader. Open your eyes to people you wouldn't normally talk to and don't be afraid to "make the ask."

Create clear communication
If you find yourself in a conversation with a potential leader, do you have something you could send them on the spot to give them a glimpse of the role? Whether it's in writing, a print piece, or a QR code linking them to a website, have information at the ready to share with a potential volunteer. Sending them the vision, the commitment, and the process might be just the tipping point you need to help someone join your team.

Form a pitch
Most people don't think of themselves as qualified to disciple teenage girls, giving excuses like "I am not cool enough" or "I don't know enough about the Bible" or "I don't think teenagers would like me." Form a sixty-second pitch to help people break down any of their preconceived notions about discipleship.

LAST THOUGHTS

As you think about assembling your team of volunteers, take a moment to reflect on yourself as a teenager. What kinds of adults did you need in your life? It's always good to put yourself in the shoes of the students in your ministry, because you were them at one point. You used to be a shy seventh grader, or a curious ninth grader, or an outspoken twelfth grader. How would you have benefitted from seeing the same leader every week? How would hearing an encouraging word from your leader have made you feel? In our need to fill volunteer spots it can be tempting to say yes to someone who might be a wonderful person but not the right fit for your ministry. Prayerfully approach recruiting volunteers and be intentional about the people you are placing in the lives of your girls.

Chapter Eight:
The Role of the Disciplemaker

Over the years, I have had many moments in youth ministry when I thought I was doing something right, but in reality was completely missing the mark. Moments when I had good intentions, but my execution led to terrible outcomes.

Please tell me you can relate. Years ago, I had a new leader named Diane join our middle school ministry team. It was her first time leading in any kind of youth ministry space and she was going to play the role of girls connect group leader—someone who leads six to eight students for ten minutes at the beginning of our youth service—at our Sunday morning service. Her previous experience was prison ministry, so naturally, I thought she was perfect to serve with middle schoolers. When Diane and I met, I told her to come on Sunday and I would give her everything she needed to jump into her new role.

When Diane showed up that first Sunday, I greeted her at the door and asked her if she was ready to jump in with eighth grade girls. She said she was feeling a little nervous and unsure of what she was supposed to do. I smiled and kind of brushed her comment off, telling her she would do great. She asked, "What should I do?" and I responded with, "Why don't you go *be relational* with students and then take this sheet of questions for group time?" She looked at me a little hesitantly and then took the questions. I told her very nonchalantly to "just jump in" and do awesome youth ministry. (I am cringing as I flash back to this moment.)

At the end of the service, Diane came up to me looking a little haggard. Like she had *seen some things,* you know? I asked her how it went, and

Disciplemaking with Girls

with a glazed look her response was, "I don't know." She said, "You told me to go be relational, but I have no idea what that means or how to do that. And then I tried to lead the girls through the questions on the sheet, but nobody would sit in the circle and the girls kept answering questions that I wasn't asking. I am not sure we talked about anything remotely spiritual."

I immediately felt so embarrassed. Here was a new leader, giving her time to disciple girls, and I didn't give her any support or training to help her win in her role. I assumed she knew what to do and sent her off without much to go on. I apologized and told her I would love to sit with her and help her get a better understanding of her role. Diane kindly thanked me but said she didn't think she was cut out for this. Our conversation ended with her telling me, "I think I am going to return to prison ministry."

There are moments in this story that make me laugh and moments that make me cringe. To this day, I giggle about Diane thinking prison ministry was easier than middle school ministry. Given a choice between a circle of eighth grade girls and a circle of reformed prisoners, she chose the latter. I also cringe looking back, because here I was thinking I was doing a great job of helping her jump into middle school ministry, when in reality I totally failed at equipping her for what she'd be doing. She had no idea what her role was or what she was supposed to do. I told her to go "be relational" and then asked her to jump into the deep end with no floatation device.

Even though this was a tough moment, I am grateful it happened. This interaction helped me become more intentional about helping leaders understand their role and how to win in that role. After what happened I started creating job descriptions for the different areas of our ministry in hopes of helping leaders feel confident and equipped to do what we were asking of them.

I don't completely know why Diane struggled that Sunday morning, but I do know if she had a greater understanding of her role, she might have felt differently about her experience. She might still have left for prison ministry, but at least I would have known it wasn't because I didn't do everything I could to help her win.

The Role of the Disciplemaker

Discipling teenage girls is an important job. When we invite leaders into this role, we need to communicate its significance. There is nothing casual or nonchalant about it. This role requires leaders to step into relational discipleship and life-on-life ministry. It's crucial that we take the time to create a thoughtful picture of the role so leaders understand what to do and what's expected. A well-considered description communicates value and care. It says to leaders, "What you are doing is important and I want you to feel confident in the role you are playing." It also communicates that we want leaders to succeed in their role—because a leader succeeding in this role equates to potential life change for a teenage girl.

If we view disciplemaking as an important job, we need to take the time to create the pathway to success. That starts with shaping the role. There are a few questions I believe it helps to ask ourselves. Although you'll likely want to approach this with some variations for your particular setting, there are three broad questions that shape the role of disciplemaker for teenage girls in most ministry settings.

- Who do we want leaders to **BE**?
- What do we want leaders to **DO**?
- How do leaders **WIN**?

JOB DESCRIPTION PART 1: WHO DO WE WANT LEADERS TO BE?

It is typically easiest to start with "what to do" when shaping a job description. But when it comes to discipleship, I think the best place to start is with who we want leaders *to be*. We need to look at the parts of the role that are not connected to a checklist of "to dos" but to a mindset and a heart posture.

Here are a few ideas you could use in this area of the job description.

A disciple
Definition: a follower or student of a teacher[12]

"If you don't have a teacher, you can't have a disciple." This quote from Dallas Willard emphasizes the importance of personal discipleship. A heart for Jesus that is pursuing, learning, loving, and following is crucial to the role of discipling teenage girls. The essence of making

Disciplemaking with Girls

disciples is our own personal discipleship pouring out into the lives around us. Prioritizing and valuing our personal relationship with Jesus has a huge impact on what can happen in a discipleship relationship with a teenage girl.

A shepherd
Definition: a person who tends and rears sheep[13]
The role of shepherd is simple: Tend the sheep God entrusts to you. A shepherd guides her sheep, looks out for her sheep, and cares for her sheep. A relational disciple is a trusted leader who shows up consistently, offers guidance, shows empathy, and walks with a girl in her struggles.

A teacher
Definition: a person who teaches[14]
I love this definition. It's like, *No duh—a teacher teaches*. But the thing to know is, the role of teacher is important. A disciplemaker teaches girls the ways of Jesus. They help girls become biblically literate. They educate girls on what it means to be a follower of Jesus. They teach truth that strengthens belief. They teach girls to love and honor Scripture. They teach girls how to question and move through doubt. They ultimately help girls become stronger disciples by expanding their knowledge of God.

A navigator
Definition: a person who directs the route or course[15]
At some point, all girls will hit hard things, whether that is pain, grief, mental health struggles, being caught in sin, or just the ups and downs of life. It can be easy to want to "fix" things or "problem-solve," but that's not a disciplemaker's role. Disciplemakers are navigators. A navigator comes alongside a girl and helps her make her way through life's tough stuff. A navigator points a girl to help. A navigator encourages new paths. A navigator points the way to resources. A navigator stands with a girl no matter how long the tough circumstances last. It's in the navigation of daily life that a girl becomes a stronger disciple of Jesus.

The Role of the Disciplemaker

A directional guide
Definition: a person who advises or shows the way to others
The process of becoming like Jesus always has a "next step" attached. This role is all about directing girls to what's next. Where can we point them to a new area of growth? Where can we encourage them to be the hands and feet of Jesus? Are they ready to share their story with others? Is there a certain book in the Bible that would be good to study next? Where can we encourage them to take a next step, maybe responding to a ministry calling or serving in kids ministry? A directional guide points out the opportunities for growth as a disciple.

This content is meant to spark your own ideas. Based on your context or your setting, you will likely add to and subtract from what's listed here.

JOB DESCRIPTION PART 2: WHAT DO WE WANT LEADERS TO DO?

This part of the job description is built on the "nuts and bolts" of the role. What do you actually want a leader to do? What are the responsibilities, expectations, and time commitment? It might feel silly to construct a job description in detail, but it's worth it. Going back to Diane, she needed me to define the word "relational." In retrospect I realize "relational" is a weird churchy word that's normal to an insider, but not to someone new. It's important to communicate the small things and the big things of the discipleship role to help minimize any questions or confusion a new leader might have.

Here are a few categories with questions attached that could help you shape this area of the job description.

Time
Helping a leader understand the time commitment helps them plan and prepare for their role. You can't show up to disciple girls if you don't know when to be there. Also, honoring someone's time is an act of care. It communicates the value you place on the time they are giving to serve in this capacity.

Questions to ask yourself
- What time of year does this commitment start and when does it end?

Disciplemaking with Girls

- What kind of weekly, monthly, and yearly time does this discipleship role require?
- Are there any trainings or gatherings or information meetings leaders need to attend?
- Are there expectations of extra time for this role outside the program, group, or church setting?

Sample breakdown of required time:
- Wednesday nights/6:30-9 p.m. (small group time w/girls: 7-8:30)
- Groups meet September-May (summer break: June-August)
- Four leader development nights each year (training, connection w/ other leaders, resources)
- Two leader check-in phone calls each year
- Outside relational time with girls in your group (four to six hours per month)

Responsibilities

Helping a leader understand their responsibilities enables them to complete the tasks that are crucial to discipleship. For some leaders, making disciples is intuitive. Others might need a detailed map to get where you want them to go. Also, if you have more than one leader discipling girls, it's nice to map out the journey you want everyone to go on to ensure that everyone is on the same page.

Questions to ask yourself

- What kind of conversations do you want happening between girls and leaders?
- Is there specific content you want them to talk about, study, learn, etc.?
- Is there any preparation required for the discipleship time together?
- Does a leader need to write or create any content?
- Does a leader need to teach any content?
- What kind of plans or calendar do you want leaders to make?
- Do you want a leader to prioritize any kind of experiences or activities for the girls they are discipling?

The Role of the Disciplemaker

Sample list of responsibilities:
- Lead spiritual conversations based on the provided content weekly
- Serve together once a month
- Have dinner together once a month
- Read through the book of John together
- Communicate with parents weekly
- Follow up with a weekly text message
- Write a weekly Bible study

The following is an example of responsibilities for one of the discipleship roles in my ministry.

Sunday Service Leader Role[16]

Before the service:	In connect groups:	During the service:
Arrive 20 minutes before the service begins	**Arrange** your circle/seating in a way that engages everyone in your group	Sit in a section with students from your group and participate in singing, games, videos, sermon, etc.
Wear your ministry shirt and grab your name tag	**Learn names** of new people, go over names of those who are back, and greet everyone–our goal is to know every student's name	**During the message:** Help students particiapte in the service
Pick up your leader instructions sheet in your connect group tub and familiarize yourself with the activity and questions		It's okay to tell students to be quiet if they are distracting those around them.
Be a master greeter, be available for conversations, be on the lookout for new students/loners, new parents	**Lead** a variety of activities, games, announcements, and icebreakers–the purpose of this time is to connect with students	**Leadership reminders:** These groups depend on your presence. Please communicate with me if you are going to miss your regularly scheduled service.
High fives, handshakes, smiles, and eye contact	**Ask** the questions and take the time to engage in spiritual conversations	
Help create an atmosphere that is warm and inviting for all students		And remember you could be a student's only connection to Jesus or a caring adult all week.

Disciplemaking with Girls

Leadership expectations
Is there anything worse than unspoken expectations? No, there is not.

Okay, I admit there actually are worse things, but unspoken expectations are pretty bad. Verbalizing discipleship expectations helps a leader be at their most effective. When expectations are communicated well, it helps a leader be at their best and ultimately win in their role.

Questions to ask yourself
- What are the things that you expect from a leader doing relational discipleship?
- Are there certain standards you are trying to uphold for leaders?
- Are there any policies you expect a leader to uphold?
- Is there something you don't want a leader to do?
- What actions or characteristics will help leaders win in their role?

Sample list of expectations:
- Commit to what you've committed to
- Comply with ministry policies and standards
- Leader first, friend second
- Value personal discipleship
- Attend leader team nights
- Communicate absences
- Seek help when you need it
- Don't do illegal stuff
- Prioritize church attendance/participation

There are all sorts of questions you can use to shape this area of the job description. These are just a few meant to spark some ideas. Based on your context or your setting, you might have some specific things that shape what or how a leader disciples a girl.

JOB DESCRIPTION PART 3: HOW DO LEADERS WIN?
This last part of the job description covers things for leaders to lean into and participate in to help win in their role.

The Role of the Disciplemaker

Leaders win when they are encouraged.
There is no such thing as too much encouragement for a leader of teenage girls. Discipleship can be a mixed bag. One moment it is rewarding and wonderful and the next it is discouraging and thankless. Leaders need ongoing encouragement to help them win in their discipleship role.

Ways to encourage
- Pay attention to your leaders' life events—milestones, birthdays, and life moments
- Have parents write notes to leaders thanking them
- Affirm small victories and big victories with cards, food, small gifts

Leaders win when they are coached.
Every leader will hit a moment in their disciplemaking journey when they need help, guidance, or coaching. Leaders need to know they are not alone and where they can go for help. A safe sounding board who is also wise in the way of discipleship is often just what a leader needs.

Ways to coach
- Create a culture where everyone on your team knows they can and should ask for help when things get tough or guidance is needed
- Find a few "mentor leaders" who can operate as wise sages for leaders doing relational discipleship
- Connect leaders to one another for peer coaching and idea sharing

Leaders win when they are equipped.
Once leaders know their job description, they will need the tools and resources to help them carry out the role. Leaders need training for discipling teenage girls. The more they know about their audience, leading, and helping girls become disciples, the easier it will be to win in their discipleship role.

Ways to equip
- Provide leaders with an overview of what it's like to be a teenage girl (like the first few chapters of this book)
- Offer training for every role in your ministry (camp counselor,

small group leader, mentor, etc.)
- Help your leaders have an understanding of youth culture/trends
- Talk through different scenarios teenage girls face (*more to come here—we are going to deep dive into training in the next chapter*)

Leaders win when they are part of a community.
Leadership can be lonely at times. Disciplemakers need a community of co-laborers. Something special happens when a community of leaders stands shoulder to shoulder in their ministry to girls. It's just a win.

Ways to build community
- Eat food together and share stories
- Meet regularly with other leaders
- Give leaders matching t-shirts (nothing says "we are in this together" like matching shirts in a terrible color)

Again, depending on your setting or context there could be more to this list.

LAST THOUGHTS
Since we eat, breathe, and sleep youth ministry, it can be easy to forget that not everyone who signs up to volunteer already knows what to do. It's our job to set our leaders up for success, and that requires clear and consistent communication. When our leaders know what is expected of them, and when they know they have a team of people supporting them, disciplemakers can walk confidently into unfamiliar spaces. I encourage you to use the guides provided in this chapter to evaluate your leader expectations and think about how you communicate those expectations to them. They are a crucial part of our ministry and it's important we give them every opportunity to win in their role.

Chapter Nine: Equipping Leaders to Make Disciples

When I first started out in youth ministry in 1996, I had no idea what I was doing. I had a calling from God and a heart for teenagers, but I didn't know much else. When I look back at those early days of my ministry career, it's like looking at the wild west of youth ministry. I didn't have a cell phone and email was just becoming a new way of communication. The internet was barely a thing and to add graphics to something I cut pictures out of books and glued them to a document. (I literally feel like I am 100 years old writing this). Most of the things I am writing in this book I learned the hard way. Most days I felt insecure and wondered if I was "doing it right."

There are so many resources, books, websites, podcasts, and videos out there today that I wish existed when I started out, things that might have made me more equipped and confident to play my ministry role earlier in my career.

The truth is, the more equipped a leader is, the more confident they feel.

Once we build a team of leaders and give them a clear job description, it's time to train and equip them to do the job. Don't leave leaders to sink or swim in relational discipleship. Leaders often feel unsure of where to start, intimidated, or wonder if they know what they are doing. Creating a plan that includes initial training, ongoing training, resources, and tools will ensure that leaders feel confident to play their role as disciplemakers.

Disciplemaking with Girls

WHY EQUIP LEADERS FOR THE ROLE OF DISCIPLEMAKER?

It's important to prepare leaders for the ministry ahead. Every disciplemaker needs ongoing training, resources, and encouragement to thrive in their role. Throwing a leader into relational discipleship without preparation and training is like sending them into the game with no equipment, instructions, or coaching.

Equipping leaders...

...prepares them for discipleship. Discipleship requires preparation. Giving leaders the opportunity to prepare their heart, schedule, mind, content, and soul is crucial to their being equipped for the journey ahead.

...shows them that their role is valuable. Time and effort scream, "I value this." Where we spend our time typically communicates what we value the most. When we take the time to train and equip leaders for discipleship, we communicate that their time and effort with teenage girls is valuable.

...communicates the importance of a "learner" attitude. The most effective leaders are always learning and growing as disciples and in their role of disciplemaking with teenage girls. Ongoing learning opportunities communicate the importance of growth.

...helps them be at their most effective. Giving every leader a clear understanding of their role and responsibilities and refining the skills they need will enhance their confidence and overall effectiveness.

Taking the time to equip yourself or equip other leaders for disciplemaking is crucial to success. And remember, success means girls becoming stronger disciples of Jesus.

WHEN DO WE EQUIP LEADERS FOR THEIR ROLE AS DISCIPLEMAKER?

The most important thing when it comes to equipping leaders is that you actually do it. In my ministry setting, the amount of time we spend on equipping leaders isn't always the same from year to year. Calendar, time, need, and numerous other factors shape how often you'll meet. The key is that leaders need consistent opportunities to learn and grow.

Equipping Leaders to Make Disciples

Only you know how often you or the other leaders you lead need to be equipped. Here are some general guidelines to help you answer the question, "How often should I equip leaders?"

Equip leaders annually

- Offer one good rally point to "kick off" new discipleship relationships, small groups, or other avenues for discipleship. Think about this like the start of a new season.
- This annual gathering for equipping and training is a great opportunity for leaders to connect with a theme, vision, or purpose for the year.
- This is a good time for leaders to start their new commitment or renew their commitment for another cycle.
- This is also a change for leaders to collect resources, content, or materials that they need for discipleship.

Equip leaders quarterly

- Choose a few key times in the year to equip leaders for their ongoing discipleship journey with girls. (This can often be planned around transition times and/or seasonal points in the calendar.)
- Quarterly trainings and gatherings are perfect opportunities to encourage leaders (think Christmas or end-of-year appreciation).
- These are good times to share stories, testimonies, new learnings, and other information that could be helpful for a leader.
- Quarterly gatherings are also when you can assess the needs of leaders and girls to better understand what future training and equipping need to happen.

Equip leaders weekly

- Provide self-directed resources so a leader can equip themselves as needed. Consider books, podcasts, apps, articles, sermons, websites. There are so many resources out there that can help leaders grow. Never before have we had so many tools at our fingertips to help us make disciples.
- Provide a sage sounding board. Every leader will need specialized coaching or equipping depending on the girls entrusted to them. Working with teenage girls is no joke. As leaders walk with girls,

they might need a coach or a mentor or someone with sage wisdom to encourage and guide them. This doesn't need to be anything formal, but it is a wonderful thing to provide for them.

Equip leaders for specific roles
- This is typically seasonal equipping to prepare leaders for a specific role that promotes disciplemaking. So, *when* you equip leaders is connected to that specific occurrence.
- This could mean equipping leaders to disciple at camps, retreats, special events, small groups, mission trips, or other areas specific to your context.
- The level of commitment and intensity of the role should dictate how robust the training is. Equipping a leader for camp might look different in time spent and how in-depth training and equipping are than what you do to prep and equip leaders for be a Friday night girls event.

HOW DO WE EQUIP LEADERS FOR THEIR ROLE AS DISCIPLEMAKER?
There are many ways to equip yourself or a team of leaders for making disciples. I want to give you three areas to think about.

Equip leaders through encouraging personal discipleship
One of the ways we can equip leaders is by encouraging them to pursue their own personal discipleship. How do we help leaders themselves grow closer to Jesus so they are in a place to help girls grow closer to Jesus?

Check in
Taking time with leaders to ask questions and check in on the condition of their heart communicates care and the importance of personal discipleship. (This isn't meant to feel like a checklist for "good Christians"—these conversations help grow relationships and lead to personal growth. The following list is just to get you thinking. Create your own list based on what's helpful for the leaders in your setting.)

Sample questions:
- How are things with your heart and soul?

Equipping Leaders to Make Disciples

- How is your connection with Jesus? What does your relationship with Jesus look like? How are you pursuing Jesus?
- What is God showing you or teaching you right now?
- Ask about struggles, doubts, or questions.
- Check in to see if leaders are participating in the adult body of the church.
- Ask about how things are going with spiritual disciplines: rest/sabbath, retreat, growing in knowledge.

When you approach these "check-ins," think about ways to create a safe space for vulnerability and authenticity. These conversations are not meant to be checking up on someone. They are opportunities to be the church and truly care for how people are doing.

Follow up
When you know how a leader needs encouragement in their personal discipleship, be sure to follow up.
- Write a card or send a text, DM, or email with encouragement.
- Pray. Text a prayer. Commit to praying.
- Circle back with accountability or an encouraging word.
- Share resources such as a helpful podcast, a website, a Bible reading plan, a worship song, or a book.

Equip leaders through community
Leaders can feel more equipped for their role when they get to rub shoulders with other leaders who do the same thing. When we provide opportunities for leaders to be in community, we create true "iron sharpening iron" spaces.

Community provides opportunities to equip leaders through…
- Encouragement
- Idea sharing
- Celebration stories
- Group learning
- Praying together
- Processing tough topics/questions

Disciplemaking with Girls

- Feeling less alone in your role. (Yes, this is equipping. Sometimes knowing others are on the journey too helps you feel more confident in your role.)

The following is a sample agenda of a community-building night with my leaders. In our ministry we call these "team nights," and they happen once a quarter. I work hard to plan and prepare these nights because they communicate value, equip leaders for their role, and create a space for leaders to connect with one another. We always try to have a little bit of everything:

- A little bit of encouragement for the soul
- A little bit of connection
- A little bit of training
- A little bit of food
- A resource to help in their role

Sample Leader Training Agenda
7:00-8:30 p.m./November

THEME: Fall
- Decorate the table(s) with fall colors, fall stuff, pumpkins, weird gourds, candy

FOOD: Anything pumpkin spice, pie, cider, coffee

ELEMENT OF FUN: GAME: Chewed candy
Hosts chew up candy and spit it out on a plate. Guess the candy. The one who gets the highest score gets a prize.

TABLE TALK: Questions/prompts to help leaders connect with one another

SOMETHING FOR THE SOUL: Encouraging the heart of a leader
- Ephesians 3:14-20
- Interactive prayer element

TRAINING: Equipping leaders for disciplemaking
- Intentional conversations
- Care and crisis for teenage girls
- Roleplay with specific scenarios

Equipping Leaders to Make Disciples

> **RESOURCES:** Sending leaders with a resource to help them in their role
> - Guide to the community–the available resources for families in need of care
>
> **COACHING TIPS:** Two tricks and tips for weekend leaders/life group leaders[17]

Equip leaders through intentional training

What kind of training does a leader need to disciple teenage girls? Whew, that feels like a big question with a very long answer. Let's face it, ministry to girls is complex. There are many different training pieces or resources that could be helpful for a leader. Start by thinking of relational discipleship and the leader job description you created. Where can you be intentional about providing training or resources?

Gather or create...
- Training that teaches a skill
- Training that shows how to play the role
- Training that provides direction/casts vision
- Training that gives talking points or language in a tough area
- Training for specific events, camps, or retreats
- Training that teaches how to navigate content
- Training that teaches different Bible study methods

Because there are so many different areas where leaders can benefit from intentional training, it's wise to think through what training you'd like to offer, like:
- Training that is vital to relational discipleship
- Training best done in community
- Training that is self-directed/self-taught
- Training that would be wonderful to eventually get to

One of the best things about equipping leaders in today's world is that there are so many resources designed for this purpose. It's also true that

Disciplemaking with Girls

depending on your context, there are training pieces you might need to create yourself. But don't waste too much time here, and don't reinvent the wheel. There are great resources available (including free ones). I am also including five different trainings I created for my leaders in the pages ahead. I have used these repeatedly throughout the years. Please feel free to use or adapt these.

In the following pages are some training samples designed to equip leaders for different parts of the disciplemaking journey, covering

- Encouragement
- Leading small group conversations
- Intentional discipleship conversations
- Building relationships
- Real-life scenarios

Training Topic: Encouragement

PURPOSE: This training is designed to give leaders practical ways to encourage girls in their discipleship journey. The sample is something you can provide to your leaders. Encouragement can be a powerful tool to help a girl become a stronger disciple of Jesus.

10 WAYS TO ENCOURAGE A TEENAGE GIRL

1. TEXT AN ENCOURAGING VERSE.
It's amazing how uplifting reminders from God's Word can be in a girl's life. Send your favorite promises or a verse that speaks to a specific situation.

"Come to me, all you who are weary and burdened, and I will give you rest. Take my yoke upon you and learn from me, for I am gentle and humble in heart, and you will find rest for your **souls**. For my yoke is easy and my burden is light." —Matthew 11:28-30 (NLT)

"**Jesus** looked at them and said, 'With man this is impossible, but not with **God**; all things are possible with **God**.'" —Mark 10:27 (NIV)

2. WRITE A NOTE AND MAIL IT.
Getting something in the mail is like winning the lottery. A note always

feels like a gift. Send a handwritten card and candy and it can completely brighten someone's day. A birthday card can also be a huge uplifter in a student's life.

3. SEND AN AUDIO TEXT WITH AN ENCOURAGING MESSAGE.
Spend ten seconds saying encouraging words, singing a song, or telling a girl to "Have a great day!"

4. PORCH-DROP.
Turn ding-dong-ditching into encouragement! Leave a treat, a note, or a group inside joke on the porch of your student's home. After you leave, text your girl so she walks out to the porch to grab it. Good surprises always fill the soul!

5. TEXT A PRAYER.
Whether it's based on a prayer request or it's something God put on your heart, type out a prayer and send it to one of your girls. Prayer has the power to encourage in really big ways.

6. SET UP FACETIME ONE-ON-ONES.
Set up a time in the week to connect over Facetime with a specific agenda. Tell your girls you would love to talk for fifteen minutes, and then make that time about them. Ask open-ended questions, ask about family, ask about friends, ask how you can be praying!

7. SEND A STARBUCKS GIFT CARD OR A SPECIFIC DIGITAL GIFT CARD.
This could serve as a promise for a future hang-out or a little surprise pick-me-up gift!

8. TEXT A JOKE.
Nothing lifts the soul like a little bit of humor. Make one of your girls laugh and see them uplifted for the rest of the week!

9. RECORD A FUNNY VIDEO AND SEND IT.
Speak life-affirming words. Tell them what they are and how they live out those qualities in good ways. Or just make a video of yourself dancing… that could be life-changing for a student. And super encouraging.

10. PUT TOGETHER A CARE PACKAGE.
Who wouldn't want to receive a tangible box of encouragement? Doesn't have to be expensive to be meaningful. Think a favorite box of cereal, favorite candy, a note card, etc.[18]

Disciplemaking with Girls

Training Topic:
Tips for Leading Small Group Conversations

PURPOSE: This training is designed to give your leaders tips on guiding girls in conversation in a small group setting. For leaders who are new to discipleship, this gives some starting points and prompts to help them be intentional in this kind of space.

LEADING & TEACHING YOUR SMALL GROUP

Create an atmosphere for conversation
- Arrive on time so you are not rushed and are ready to receive girls when they arrive.
- Create an atmosphere where girls can focus and be present.
- Prep the space with comfortable seating arranged for conversation.
- Prepare group materials, conversation prompts, and content before girls arrive.
- Have extra group materials, Bibles, and snacks in case a girl forgets (or shows up after basketball).
- Ask girls to put their cell phones on silent when they arrive (or create a cell phone bucket).

Make the content your own
- Read the weekly conversation guide before you arrive at group. Think about your group of girls and what pieces of the content are most relevant and most helpful for them.
- Make notes and feel the freedom to go above and beyond the guide. Remember that girls learn and comprehend things in different ways: visually, verbally, through hands-on experience, etc. Think about tangible experiences, spiritual tangents, or elements of fun that will give girls the opportunity to not just listen but participate.
- Gather materials, test videos, and buy any necessary supplies.
- Pay attention to the group response. When you are leading, ask yourself questions like, "How are my girls responding to the conversation?" "Is it over their head?" "Is it challenging enough?" "Are they participating?" "Are they interested in the topic?"

Equipping Leaders to Make Disciples

Think experiential
- Experiences help content stick. Think through ways to take the content and conversation from page to practical.
- Take one thing from the content and create an experience around it. For example, if the topic is prayer, think of creating a few prayer stations around the room.

Tips for conversation
- Don't talk too much, allow students to participate, ask questions, and process. Think 70/30: The leader talking 30% of the time and girls talking 70% of the time.
- Silence is not a bad thing. Sometimes girls need a little time to think before they answer.
- Read through any Bible passages two or three times. Give students plenty of time to listen and grasp what is meaningful.
- Encourage girls to highlight, underline, or circle key words and verses in their Bible.
- Utilize the memory verses, practices, experiences, and next steps in each conversation guide.
- Fun can be a door that leads to deeper conversation. Don't be afraid to include laughter, games, and fun to build trust and relax the girls.[19]

Training Topic: Intentional Discipleship Conversations

PURPOSE: This training is designed to give leaders prompts and questions that lead to intentional discipleship conversations with teenage girls.

POINT, PURSUE, AND PRACTICE

Reminders before you have intentional conversations with girls

Create a safe space
- It gives girls permission to be vulnerable
- It sets the stage for honesty and transparency

Every conversation sets up the next one
- Be aware of your face, your body language, and your tone
- It's okay to say, "I don't know, but let's circle back about this"

Disciplemaking with Girls

You are on a journey
- You don't need to squeeze everything into one conversation

Think about planting seeds for the future: after the conversation, give a next step
- Follow up

How do we have conversations that POINT girls to Jesus?

How do we point a girl to Jesus in her daily life?
- When she needs encouragement, how can we point her to Scripture, prayer, and promises?
- When she needs guidance or direction, how can we point her to Jesus for answers?
- When she needs to understand truth, how can we point her to God's words, voice, and perspective?

How do we have conversations that help girls PURSUE Jesus?

How do we help a girl pursue her own discipleship?
- When she has big questions, how can we teach her to ask Jesus first? How do girls form habits of pursuit if we answer all the questions?
- When she wants to grow in her relationship with Jesus, how can we help her pursue different avenues to connect with him?
- When culture says something different from what God says, how do we help a girl pursue truth?
- Where do we tell girls to go with their questions? Where do we look together?

How do we have conversations to help girls PRACTICE following Jesus?

How do we help a girl practice following Jesus every day?
- Read through a book of the Bible together
- Pray with one another
- Sing a worship song together
- Serve together
- Do random act of kindness together
- Go through a Bible reading plan together
- Attend church together
- Take communion together

Following Jesus shoulder to shoulder can have a powerful impact on a teenage girl.

Equipping Leaders to Make Disciples

Training Topic: Building Relationships

PURPOSE: This training is designed to help leaders build meaningful relationships with teenage girls. With relational discipleship being the primary youth ministry strategy, this is an important place for every leader to invest their time.

BUILDING RELATIONSHIPS WITH TEENAGE GIRLS

CREATE MEMORABLE MOMENTS
We as leaders need to venture beyond programmed settings to build relationships with girls. The smallest gestures can begin the building process and set you on a path toward strong discipleship relationships.

IDEAS:
- Go to her world. Take part in a girl's life outside of your scheduled time. Attend a sporting event, band performance, speech meet, play, etc.
- Create "remember that time" memories. ("Remember that time we went to the grocery store in our pajamas?")
- Make a fun sign, decorate your car, attend tryouts, make a big deal of what is happening in her world.

INTENTIONAL FOCUSED CONVERSATION
As leaders, we need to seek out intentional conversations with girls. Engaging in meaningful conversations can set girls on a course toward deeper relationships with you and with Jesus.

IDEAS:
- Remove distraction. Pick a spot to talk where others won't break your focus.
- Listen and maintain good eye contact. Make sure your cell phone is put away and don't look at your watch.
- Just listen, don't try to fix. Work to respond with a related question so a girl knows you were listening.
- Point them to a resource (if applicable): a book, a podcast, a song, or something that directly relates.
- Follow up with next steps or encouragement.

MAXIMIZE YOUR LIMITED TIME
As leaders, we have limited time to disciple girls each week. Make the most of it!

Disciplemaking with Girls

IDEAS:
- Invite girls into your life. They don't care what you do, they just want to spend time together. (Think grocery shopping, errands, or getting something to eat.)
- Make the most of your scheduled time together. Be on time and have a plan.
- Be strategic about connecting with a specific girl each week.

LEAD THEM TOWARD NEXT STEPS WITH JESUS
As leaders, we have a unique opportunity to give spiritual encouragement and direction.

IDEAS:
- Ask about their relationship with Jesus. Listen and give ideas for next steps based on the answer.
- Expose them to the Bible, podcasts, apps, sermons, and/or music that could help them grow in their relationship with Jesus. What is God showing you that you could pass on?
- Is there a practice to encourage? Worship, serving, memorizing Scripture, building community?

Training Topic: Student Scenarios

PURPOSE: This training is designed to allow leaders to have conversations around different scenarios that could surface in their relationship with teenage girls. As we work to help girls become stronger disciples of Jesus, training like this can help leaders to be more thoughtful and intentional in their responses to what comes up.

Teenage Girl Scenarios
Give each leader a set of "scenario cards." This training can be done as a group exercise with a table of leaders, or as an individual exercise for one specific leader. Take time to talk through every scenario.

Starter questions:
- What is the girl feeling in this scenario?
- How do we respond?
- What thoughtful language do we use in our response?
- What should our tone, body language, and facial expression be like?
- What kind of next steps would we offer?

A girl wants to give her life to Jesus and she asks you what to do.	A girl tells you she doesn't believe in Jesus anymore. How do you respond?	A mom calls you to let you know her daughter is struggling with depression.
You have a girl who really loves Jesus and wants to grow in her relationship with him. Where do you point her first?	A girl tells you she has had suicidal thoughts lately.	A girl believes God is calling her into a life of ministry. How do you help her explore that calling?
A girl tells you she is having sex with her boyfriend.	A girl tells you she is struggling with her identity.	Two girls in your small group are not speaking to each other and it is creating divisiveness among the rest of the group.

LAST THOUGHTS

I can't help but think back to twenty-one-year-old Katie Edwards. She needed this chapter. She needed someone encouraging her to keep pursuing her own personal relationship with Jesus. She needed a community to grow with, lean on, and learn from. She needed intentional training that helped her feel more confident in her relational discipleship role. I keep thinking to myself, "Gosh, I wish I had this twenty-five years ago."

I know this was a lot to take in—but I also know that this could be helpful for a leader just like me.

Part Three:
THE INGREDIENTS THAT MAKE UP A DISCIPLE

Disciplemaking with GIRLS

One of my favorite things to bake is chocolate chip cookies. I think it's because I know the recipe by heart, and also because, is there anything better than warm chocolate chip cookies out of the oven? Anyway, the most important thing in baking is getting the ingredients just right. In fact, that's crucial to the end result. Add a little too much of one thing or not enough of another and it throws off the whole batch. But when you put in just the right mix of ingredients you get magic melting in your mouth.

I think this is the perfect analogy for making disciples with teenage girls. There are some crucial ingredients that help put a girl on the trajectory toward becoming a devoted disciple of Jesus.

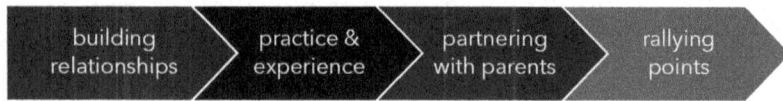

Now, this is not meant to be a pathway or stepping stones to making disciples. Think of these as ingredients that you toss in the bowl and mix. Too much of one thing and not enough of another might alter the journey. But the right mix of ingredients working together will produce the best end result. There are a variety of ingredients that can help girls become like Jesus, but in the chapters ahead I want to focus on these four:

INGREDIENT 1: BUILDING RELATIONSHIPS
The starting point for relational discipleship is taking the time to build relationships and deepen trust.

INGREDIENT 2: PRACTICE AND EXPERIENCE
Practice and experience were woven throughout Jesus's journey with the disciples. Through practice and experience we can SHOW, TEACH, GUIDE, and PREPARE girls to become like Jesus.

INGREDIENT 3: PARTNERING WITH PARENTS
Parents' influence in the life of a teenage girl is undeniable. Nothing comes close to the consistent time and space they occupy together. Girls need a bunch of people besides their parents at the discipleship table, but they also really need their parents. The partnership between parents and caring adults is what makes the biggest impact on a girl's discipleship journey.

The Ingredients That Make Up a Disciple

INGREDIENT 4: RALLYING POINTS

Disciplemaking relationships need to start somewhere. What are the rallying points—the intentional spaces designed to create connection and launch teen girls and adult leaders into relational discipleship?

These are the ingredients I believe are crucial at this stage of adolescence. As we grow as disciples over time, we'll also incorporate others. I mean, I started adding pretzels to my chocolate chip cookie recipe and it was life-changing. These are not the ONLY ingredients of making disciples, but I do believe they are the right ones to start with as we journey with teenage girls. The goal is to put them on a trajectory toward a lifelong journey with Jesus.

Chapter Ten:
Building Relationships

I met Elaina at the end of her seventh grade year. She was part of our youth ministry, well-liked by other students, involved with our student worship team, and a regular attender at church. She was a little reserved, but I caught glimpses of her energy and her smile when she was around her close friends. At the beginning of eighth grade, Elaina was assigned to be in my small group. I was excited to spend time with her and get to know her. But when we met, she seemed less excited about me. For our first small group, we did a "get to know you" type of night. I invited parents so I could connect with them as well. When Elaina walked in, I greeted her with a lot more energy than she could handle. She smiled, said hello, and then quickly walked away to connect with the other girls. (I do come on kind of strong at times...) I was a little bummed, because I really wanted to get to know her, become best friends, disciple her, get thanked for my spiritual direction in her valedictorian speech, and perform her wedding someday. What? That's a normal thought process. JK, it's nuts. But that was the energy I greeted her with when she walked in the door. My friends like to say I am an aggressive friend. In youth ministry, sometimes that serves me well and other times it does not. This was one of the latter times.

Elaina avoided me for most of that first small group night. I had a longer conversation with her parents than I did with her. That first month of small group, I tried so hard to connect with Elaina. I tried everything I knew how to do and then tried new things as well. No matter how hard I worked to engage her in conversation, I could never really get anywhere. She just seemed uninterested. It didn't help that her face was impossible to read, and she wasn't the most expressive human. I swear I could hear my insecurities scream "She hates you!"

Disciplemaking with Girls

I was so unsure of how to proceed. But God put this heavy burden for Elaina on my heart.

Have you ever felt that with a student? God gives you a burden for them and you just know he put you in each other's paths for a reason? That is what I felt when I met Elaina. And that is what motivated me to keep trying to build a relationship with her. Like I mentioned before, I saw glimpses of her laughter, her smile, and her genuine love for Jesus. But the key detail I needed to pay attention to was that Elaina was only comfortable enough to show those things when she was around people she trusted. I was not one of those people. Yet.

Fast forward into month two of our small group and the moment when everything shifted: *game night*. I invited the girls to come to my house for dinner and games. It was a loud, competitive, crazy night, but it was the lynchpin for me and Elaina. Something happened between the animated dinner conversation and the competitive rounds of a dice game called Tensies, and Elaina and I had our first relaxed, organic conversation. At the end of the night, she gave me a big hug as she walked out the door and said, "You will be at church this weekend, right?" I looked at her and said, "Yes, I will. Save me a seat." I was super calm and chill in my response, even though my insides were doing cartwheels and screaming loud things. We had a moment, and I was so excited.

I would like to tell you the next day we became besties and our discipleship journey began, but it wasn't like that. Everything with her was a slow build. It took a series of big and small moments to build a relationship with Elaina. Car rides, dinner after church, encouraging texts, and our weekly small group times all helped lay the foundation for deeper relationship and trust. I knew I wouldn't interact with the real Elaina until she trusted me. So, through a combination of fun moments, time together, proximity with one another, and shared experiences, we eventually built the trust that was needed.

Once that trust was built it led to depth in our relationship. And it was in that depth where the disciplemaking began. Elaina invited me into her life and ultimately allowed me to walk with her in her faith. She eventually felt comfortable enough to share her struggles, doubts, and questions about God. We prayed together, worshipped together, studied God's Word together, and shared life consistently. She would text me every Monday and ask me if I needed prayer and she would text me every Friday to see if I was going to church. (I would always giggle, because I don't think she knew I had to be at church—it was my job. I still appreciated the text.) She had big questions, struggled with self-worth and identity, and wrestled with her relationship with her parents. She genuinely loved Jesus, but also struggled with following him in her daily life. Every day presented new opportunities and new challenges for us to walk through together. At the beginning of my relationship with Elaina it was impossible to envision where we are now. It took about a year of planting seeds and allowing those seeds to take root to put the two of us on the path to discipleship. But gosh, every minute of seed-planting was worth it, because that time ultimately led to Elaina becoming a stronger disciple of Jesus. And the turning point was *game night*, of all things.

Relationships set the stage for making disciples. The key is understanding that building relationships is not a step taken *before* making disciples, it is part of the process.

You might be tempted to sidestep or skip this part. I get it. You want to make disciples now. But it's important to understand that strong relationships lead to deeper levels of trust, and trust is crucial to relational discipleship. On a journey with a teenage girl, trust opens doors like nothing else can.

We can see this throughout Jesus's ministry with the disciples. He built relationships with them over time through shared life, intentional moments, and experiences. Big and small moments laid the foundation for their relationship and ultimately led to deeper levels of trust.

Elaina was assigned to my small group, but her name being on my roster did not automatically jumpstart the discipleship process. I had to do the work of building a relationship with her to get to the trust that opened the door to disciple her.

Building trust cannot be rushed. It takes time, energy, and intentionality. But when trust is built, it creates space for so many wonderful things to happen.

Trust creates space for you to...
- be authentic and vulnerable with one another
- have conversations around God's perspective vs. the world's perspective
- share about your own journey and what God is teaching you
- meet a girl in her struggles with relationships, doubt, mental health, or sin
- feel permission to ask tough questions
- take opportunities to give guidance and encouragement
- listen and hear what is really going on
- have the permission to challenge thinking
- share God's voice and help a girl listen for it and recognize it in the sea of voices

So, how do we build the trust that ultimately opens the door for discipleship? Great question. There are a lot of different ways. Some are no-brainers and others require an intentional approach. I believe it is a combination of shared moments, experiences, conversations, and life together that ultimately lead to strong trust in a relationship.

In this chapter we will explore five ways to build relationships with teenage girls. Before you panic, know that you don't need to do or be good at everything in every category to be effective. I wanted to give you a lot of ideas and options in hopes that you can connect with a few things that fit with your wiring as a leader. Some categories include practical tools you can use, and others offer an overarching idea. All of them are meant to give you starting points for strengthening the relational foundation between you and the girls God entrusts to you.

#1: TIME
If we look at our schedule or our calendar, chances are high we'll see that we give a good chunk of our time to the things we value most. Now, I know I am generalizing. But *in general* when we give time to something, we are communicating that we value that thing. When we give time to a teenage girl, we are communicating that she is valuable.

It shows her that the journey of becoming like Jesus is not a waste of time but a very wise use of it. These things matter—the amount of time we set apart and give, and how we maximize our limited time when it comes to leading girls. There is more than one way to give time to a teenage girl. Not all time is the same, but all time does lead to deeper relationships.

Quality time
This is the MVP of time. I think it's because "quality" is in the title. This kind of time can happen one-on-one or in a small group setting and it's often best when it is structured. Quality time is the kind of time that is set apart and comes with a plan.

This kind of time looks like…
- Giving undivided attention
- Putting your cell phone on silent or completely away
- Body language and facial expressions that communicate attentiveness
- Significant or meaningful conversation
- Active listening
- A setting with no distractions
- Structured time with an end goal in mind
- Scheduled for an intentional length of time (when time is scheduled, it communicates commitment and value—It feels more like *quality time* when it is time intentionally set apart)

When all of this comes together for quality time, it strengthens relationships and builds trust. There is not a specific amount of time required for quality time, and it can happen as often as needed.

Quantity time
This might seem like the shallow little sister of quality time, but there is nothing shallow about quantity time. This is ANY kind of time together. It can happen one-on-one, in a small group setting, during a whole youth group together, or at a party with fifty people. There are endless possibilities for quantity time, and it is typically best when unstructured.

Disciplemaking with Girls

This kind of time looks like...
- Being present physically or digitally
- Any kind of texting or online conversation
- Car ride conversations
- Phone conversations (I think these still happen?)
- Responses, likes, and DMs on social platforms
- Asking questions and active listening
- Outings, errands, food, or fun together
- Being planned or spontaneous (you can plan to hang out without it being structured, and you can also spontaneously jump in a car after church and go grab food)

All these pieces of quantity time contribute to strengthening relationship and building trust. This kind of time should happen as often as possible. I mean, the definition is in the title...it's quantity! This kind of time unlocks pieces of relationship that quality time just doesn't always allow for. You might learn more about a girl's story in one car ride home from small group than you learned in the actual small group itself. It's the organic nature of quantity time moments that new layers of relationship are built.

Both kinds of time are equally valuable and important. Incorporating both quality time and quantity time will lead to stronger relationships with deeper levels of trust.

How much time is the right amount?
I overthink this question a lot. I wonder if I am giving enough time, if the time I am giving is worthwhile, or if I am giving too much time and neglecting other things? But what I have learned is there is no magic number of hours when it comes to time with teenage girls. There is no number of hours that ensures a girl will become a stronger follower of Jesus. I believe if you work to strike a balance between structured and unstructured time in discipleship relationships, you will find the sweet spot. Also, keep in mind that different girls and groups require different kinds of time, and the time you spend in one season might look different from the next. The right amount of time is always changing and shifting to meet the current need of the relationship.

Building Relationships

Something I come back to often in my own ministry is that God is at work in every moment. Structured or unstructured, he is always moving, and he is not limited to our sense of time. The time I give is led by him and is leading his girls toward becoming stronger disciples. It's easy to beat yourself up over time given but try to remember that every moment is movement forward and God is in it with you, leading and guiding in ways only he can.

#2: FUN
I LOVE FUN. Sooooo much. There is something magical about its power to build relationships and deepen trust. Fun is a universal language among teenagers, and it is the key to unlocking deeper relationship with girls.

Fun can be a lot of things. Some think fun is…
- something funny or amusing
- something enjoyable or light-hearted
- something wild and crazy
- something funny—sarcastic/joking/teasing
- something entertaining

Each of these ideas of fun is correct. I looked in the dictionary. Fun is so many things, but one thing it is *not* is a waste of time.

Fun is a crucial tool in relationship-building. There's a common misperception, especially in the church, that fun is pointless or that it takes away from spiritual things. But fun is a building block. While the fun itself might not have incredible depth, it can help foster an atmosphere where deeper conversations, sharing, and discipleship can happen.

When a leader comes to me and tells me they are struggling to connect or get into deeper conversation with girls, my first question is always, "When was the last time you had some fun?" Why? Well, fun has a way of relaxing an environment so that conversation flows more easily. Fun fosters connection and strengthens bonds. It can relax a girl and help create an environment where she can be herself. Fun and laughter and smiling release endorphins, which honestly just makes a girl feel good.

Disciplemaking with Girls

Fun brings lightheartedness into heavy weeks and helps lift spirits after a terrible day. Fun can lead to cry-laughing, which feels the same as taking a deep breath. Then, somehow, that cry-laughing opens a door to vulnerability and authenticity and gives permission to then weep together. That is the magic of fun. To skip the fun would be missing out on the depth it could lead to in relationships with teenage girls.

Where does the fun begin?
Below are a few starting points for thinking about fun with teenage girls.

Create a "fun" resource bank
Buy a plastic tub for games and icebreakers that can act as a go-to arsenal when you need fun things to build relationships. Label it the "fun tub"? Whew, that's super lame. But you get it.

What goes in the tub?
- Board games (Apples to Apples, Pictionary, Things)
- Card games (spicy Uno, Monopoly Deal, spoons, Play Nine)
- Icebreakers (you can literally google the word "icebreaker" and get a million options)
- A bunch of dice
- Note pads/pencils
- Small white board/markers
- Timer/buzzer

Create a list of fun places to go
What are all the fun things to do within a reasonable driving distance? Make a list of places to visit or outings to go on that will help build relationships with girls.
- Unique restaurants (including dives and hole-in-the wall places)
- Trampoline park
- Amusement park
- Mini golf
- Bowling
- Unique dessert/treat stops

- Weird or unique famous landmarks or museums ("World's largest" whatever? Yes, please.)

Create fun memories
Fun outings, occasions, and locations all act as a backdrop for powerful memory making moments that foster bonding and connection. Create fun opportunities that will eventually lead to a girl saying the phrase, "Remember that time when…?"

Ideas to create "remember that time?" moments:
- Progressive dinner
- Movie singalong
- Sunset or sunrise hike
- Choose five people to door drop fresh baked chocolate chip cookies
- Photoshoot at a famous nearby landmark
- Pictures with Santa or the Easter Bunny at the mall
- Get a manicure/pedicure (There is a local place near me that does karaoke and manicures. It is the weirdest, most hilarious thing that girls never forget.)

There are so many other ways to use fun as a tool. Remember that fun should be taken seriously. That's kind of a funny thing to say, but it's true. Fun leads to deeper relationship and trust with teenage girls.

#3: CONVERSATION
Obviously, conversation is used to build relationships with teenage girls. But I believe it's important for us to touch on this because some people are really bad at conversation. I am not pointing any fingers, I will just ask you this: Have ever been in a conversation with someone who was bad at conversation? It's not fun.

Conversation is an artform with the power to influence, guide, instruct, encourage, and correct. A meaningful conversation with a teenage girl can act as a bridge to deeper trust. Conversations create opportunities to show a girl she is loved, seen, heard, and cared for. They can challenge thinking, hold space for doubt, and operate as a platform for a deepening faith. They can point to Scripture, unlock doors to spiritual

Disciplemaking with Girls

growth, and show the way to Jesus. Conversations play an important role in helping girls become stronger disciples of Jesus, which is why it's important to be good at them.

Leading meaningful conversations

While conversations do require two-way communication (that is what makes it a conversation, after all), it is up to the leader to guide the way. Girls may or may not know how to engage in meaningful conversation. Through asking good questions, active listening, bringing up intentional talking points, and giving thoughtful responses, leaders model the power of a meaningful conversation and what it can lead to. This is the essence of relational discipleship.

Let's take a closer look at the three parts of a meaningful conversation.

Asking good questions

One of the most worthwhile skills a leader can develop is asking good questions. Questions can play a role in all parts of a conversation. They help launch conversation, they are a vessel that keeps conversation moving, and they can be a great means to end a conversation in a way that challenges thinking. Questions help us know the girls we are discipling and where they are in their journey with Jesus. Questions also encourage self-discovery, help with critical thinking, and bring about a deeper understanding of faith.

Tips to keep in mind when asking questions:

- Ask open-ended questions that require more than a yes or no answer.
- Start questions with, "Could you tell me about…?" or, "How does that work…?" to really get a girl talking.
- Don't be afraid to rephrase questions a few different ways to help a girl really understand what is being asked.
- Balance personal questions that deepen the relationship between the girl and the leader with faith-building questions that deepen her relationship with Jesus.
- Think of questions that could challenge thinking, lead to a next step, prompt a leap of faith, or encourage a deep dive into Scripture.

- Be aware that there are times to ask questions that keep things relaxed and casual and there are times to be intentional in leading toward deeper places.

Active listening
There is nothing more wonderful than an active listener. When someone gives you their full attention along with their listening ear, it is such a meaningful act of care. A leader who listens will naturally lead the conversation in a meaningful direction, acting as a safe sounding board that can hold everything a girl talks about. Only in listening to where a girl is can you respond thoughtfully, wisely, and kindly. Only in listening can you discern and respond with a prompt for a next step. Listening is a powerful piece of meaningful conversation.

When active listening:
- Maintain warm eye contact
- Remove distractions
- Relax your body and your face
- Nod your head and respond with quiet sounds to show you are with them
- Repeat back to them things that were said so they know you understand what is being shared

Thoughtful responses
One of the toughest parts of a conversation with a teenage girl is responding thoughtfully. Leaders typically have a strong urge to jump in with sage advice, "the answer" to the girl's problem, or with an attempt to fix something that's broken. Now, there is a place for a leader to offer wisdom and life learning, but that shouldn't be what they lead with. Crafting a thoughtful response with intentional talking points is crucial in the trust-building process with a teenage girl. It's in our responses that the door remains open to future conversations. It is in our responses where trust is strengthened or weakened. One wrong move and there are relational consequences.

I don't say that to scare you, but to raise awareness of how impactful our responses are. So what does responding thoughtfully look like?

Disciplemaking with Girls

Thoughtful responses are responses that convey:
- love
- grace
- respect
- an overall "safe place" vibe

It is impossible to prepare for every conversation that could come your way with a teenage girl, but there are general talking points that can work in multiple types of conversations. These talking points help keep the conversation on a meaningful track, maintain trust, and don't shut down the possibility for a next conversation.

Thoughtful responses to offer when a girl shares something with you:
- "Wow, thank you for sharing that with me. I feel honored."
- "Do I have permission to ask some questions?"
- "Do you mind if I share some thoughts with you, or would you rather I wait?"
- "Is this something you've talked with Jesus about?"
- "Is this something you would like me to check in on from time to time?"
- "What can I pray for specifically? Can we pray together right now?"
- "Can we look at Scripture together to process this?"
- "Wow, this must be so tough. How are you feeling?"

Conversations are a bridge to relationship and deeper trust with a teenage girl.

#4 PROXIMITY
This is an easy one. Just be in proximity with girls on a consistent basis and relationships will grow and trust will strengthen.

Okay? That's it for this one.

Just kidding. While the concept of proximity is simple, it still requires a certain kind of intentionality. The physical kind. What I mean by that is, this area of relationship building can only happen when you are in physical proximity with a teenage girl. The other areas rely on proximity too, but there are ways to have fun, spend time together, and have conversation that don't require physical presence with one another. The idea is not that you are present with each other 24/7. A little goes a long way. There is something special about sitting knee to knee and face to face with someone. Physical presence impacts like nothing else. When you are in proximity with a girl, she can hear the tone of your voice, she can experience warmth from your body language, she can see grace in your eyes, and she can see love in your facial expression. When I think of proximity, I think of a shepherd and a sheep. The shepherd physically looks out for his sheep and cares for his sheep. The sheep listen to the shepherd's voice and following the shepherd's lead. The sheep and shepherd have a special relationship because they exist in a physical space together. It is that presence with one another that builds relationship and deepens trust. Now, I am not suggesting that you and the girls you disciple move to a pasture together, but I am saying that the time you spend in proximity with one another can yield powerful results.

Go to a girl's world

It is amazing what can happen when you leave your typical "discipleship turf" and venture into a girl's world. Meeting a girl in her world offers a fresh perspective on who she is, and it gives you a glimpse into the spaces she is living in. Also, chances are high that her world is where she feels the most comfortable to be herself. Going to a girl's world creates a unique connection point with you and a girl that helps nudge open doors that lead to trust.

Ways to show up in a girl's world
- Attend her sporting event, drama production, or piano recital
- Pick her up from school and take her to get a treat
- Attend anything at school—play, speech meet, etc.
- Invite yourself to dinner with her family
- Ask to see drawings, art, or writing she is working on
- Comment on her social media posts

The following is a sample of a card I created to find out what events are happening in a girl's life. It's meant to give me a few starting points for

Disciplemaking with Girls

'going to her world.' I use this card to then plan ways I can spend time in proximity with each of my girls.

WHAT'S HAPPENING?

Write down some of the events upcoming in your life that are important to you (soccer games, concerts, dance recitals, drama productions, speech meets, etc.). I would love to come and support you!

Name _____

1. _____ Date _____
2. _____ Date _____
3. _____ Date _____
4. _____ Date _____
5. _____ Date _____

Invite a girl into your world

We've been talking throughout this book about sharing life with one another. So, if you are going to her world, it only makes sense that you would also invite her into yours. By inviting a girl into your world, you give her the opportunity to see how you live for Jesus in your daily life. You give her a fresh perspective on your day-to-day, the challenges faced and the joys experienced. This helps girls see that life as a grown-up still means being on a journey to becoming like Jesus. This invite can include any ordinary activity in your daily life—grocery shopping, running errands, or hanging out at your kid's soccer game. Incorporate them into parts of your life that happen whether they are there or not. Girls don't care what you are doing, they are just excited to be a part of something with you.

I invited a few girls to a worship night I was attending at our church. It wasn't geared for teenagers, but it was an opportunity for anyone in the church to connect with God through a worshipful experience. When we arrived, I could tell they were skeptical, but by the end of the night we were standing shoulder to shoulder singing our guts out. It was something I would have gone to with or without them; it was an experience that my heart needed that night. But by inviting the girls into my world, we had an experience together that ended up creating a unique disciplemaking moment. We were worshipping in proximity and the girls caught glimpses of my faith, my love for Jesus, and my worship of him. I had the opportunity, just by being myself in my world, to model something for my girls. We walked away from that night with something special, a deeper connection to Jesus and to one another. I am convinced this only happened through us existing in that physical space together. So, invite them in. Don't be afraid to be yourself and model the good, the easy, the hard, the struggle, and what it looks like to be on your own journey of becoming like Jesus.

#5: SOCIAL PLATFORMS

This might seem like a very odd suggestion for a place to build relationship and deepen trust with a teenage girl. But when we think of our audience and the level of importance social platforms hold in their lives, it makes sense to utilize social media as a tool. The truth is, girls are in this space. A lot. Social media is where they interact multiple times a day and have varying levels of relationships, from best friends to family to acquaintances to total strangers. They view these platforms as a space to "share their life" with their people. I know not everyone participates in these spaces, but if you are helping a teenage girl become a stronger disciple of Jesus, you need to join at least one social platform. Younger generations will never know a world without social media; they will grow up viewing this as a place for relationships. You don't have to like it or interact with anyone except the girls you disciple, but interacting with them over social media and social platforms is vital. This is where girls are.

What are some ways we build relationships in this space?

Follow
Following a girl on her social platform communicates you care about her life, and you are paying attention to her thoughts, feelings, and snapshots. It is an act of trust on her end to let you into this part of her world. Tapping the follow button can be a tool that deepens trust.

Let girls follow you back
By letting girls follow you, it communicates trust as well. You are inviting them into your life and giving them access to a part of your world. It shows a girl that you want to share your life with her in this space and you trust her with your thoughts, feelings, and snapshots.

Disciplemaking with Girls

Like and comment on as many things as possible
Like, comment, or subscribe to posts. Maybe not *everything*, but do it as often as you can. Likes and comments are forms of encouragement, reminders of your presence in her life, and an opportunity to disciple. I know there are statistics that point to the dark side of likes and comments and the negative things they can perpetuate. I agree that there are some unhealthy connections between social platforms and a girl's view of herself. But here we are. In the middle of this world. So how can you be a different voice that pushes against negativity and reinforces something positive? Every post is an opportunity to comment in a way that communicates something significant that strengthens relationship.

Do I like or comment on ALL pictures?
There are times when scrolling through pics in your feed when you catch a glimpse of a girl engaging in behaviors or activities that you don't necessarily want to hit the like button for. I don't love every single picture my girls post, but I love them regardless of what they post. So, I try to remember my role and comment accordingly. Working to find ways to encourage without sounding fake or coming across as judgmental. For example, I saw a post recently that was, for lack of a better phrase, a "sexy bikini photoshoot" of one of my junior girls. All the comments were about her body and how she looked. Please hear me, I have nothing against bikinis, but I knew there was a motivation behind why she posted it and what she was looking for in the comments. So, I thought about my voice and commented, "Yay for summer! So excited for bathing suit weather!" My comment stood out among the sea of comments because it was in a different tone and had a different vibe than the others. Cheesy? Yes. Effective? I think so. She gave me a heart emoji for it. All this to say, there are ways to comment and be present in a loving, encouraging way even when we don't love the content.

Be aware of etiquette on social platforms
Don't embarrass yourself.

The rules are constantly changing, so check in with the girls you are discipling for any and all updates on social media missteps.

Building Relationships

Use the platform for discipleship
There is a lot of crazy stuff on social platforms, but there are a lot of wonderful things as well. There are so many ways to be intentional here. You can send encouragement, point to a next step, and help a girl grow in her relationship with Jesus. The things you share will create points of connection between you and your girls.

You can send…

- Videos that promote good news or feel-good stories
- Scripture in all forms—text, pictures, videos
- Sermons, podcasts, or YouTube videos that point a girl to Jesus
- Inspiring stories or testimonies

LAST THOUGHTS
I started this chapter talking about Elaina, and I am going to finish by coming back to her. When I think about these five categories for connection, I see them woven throughout my relationship with her. We've spent quality and quantity time together, we've had a lot of fun together, we've found ourselves in many meaningful conversations, we've experienced the power of proximity, and we've interacted in the digital world. All of these relationship builders have led to a level of trust between us that is propelling Elaina forward in her journey to becoming like Jesus.

Relationships lead to trust and trust leads to depth. It's in the depth where disciplemaking happens.

Chapter Eleven:
Becoming Like Jesus

When I was in high school, I took Intro to Ceramics. I thought this class was going to be easy, but it turned out to be super challenging (or maybe it was just really challenging for me). One of the first assignments was to construct a water pitcher. The teacher gave us each a cube of clay, showed us ways to work with it, and gave specific instructions on how to construct a water pitcher. We were given three weeks to complete the project. In my mind I couldn't understand why it would take that long. I mean, how hard could it be?

Turns out it was very hard. To my surprise, shaping clay into a household item took large amounts of patience, time, and help. I remember vividly how closely the ceramics teacher walked with me in this particular project. She was so patient and so present. She would show me something and then sit with me while I tried it. She gave me guidance and starting points for each section and then she would let me try it for myself. She would walk by my station and ask if I needed help and offer affirmation as I completed different aspects of the project. I desperately needed her help and I wouldn't have finished the project without it. When I look back, it's clear that I would have been lost without her. She played a crucial role in helping me become the ceramics expert I am today. Just kidding, I'm really bad at it.

When I think about the role of a disciplemaker, it reminds of my ceramics teacher.

When I think about teenage girls becoming devoted disciples of Jesus, it reminds me of young Katie constructing a water pitcher.
Oh man, you might have thought I was going to work in a "potter and

Disciplemaking with Girls

clay" reference. Maybe later. Nope, this story highlights the role of the teacher and the role of the student.

Leader and disciple.

Leader: My teacher intentionally came alongside me, showed me how to shape clay, taught me how to do it, and then told me to do it on my own.

Disciple: I watched my teacher shape the clay, listened to her instructions, and then did my best to imitate what she showed me.

This is what "making disciples" looks like.

I suppose my ceramics teacher and I are not the very best example that could be used here. Let's face it, Jesus, and the way he intentionally led and developed the twelve disciples, is *the model.*

Jesus walked *with* the disciples and showed them, taught them, encouraged them, and empowered them for ministry. He was thoughtful about teaching moments, and intentional in his interactions, hands-on experiences, and practicing his own love for the Father in front of them. He invited them in, shared life with them, and prepared them for the mission ahead.

The disciples walked *with* Jesus. Followed his lead, travelled with him, shared meals, and spent time getting to know him. They listened to his teachings, watched him perform miracles, and stood by while he interacted with unlikely people. They learned new truths, they served, they ministered, they had doubts and questions, and they grew in their love and knowledge of God.

Jesus came alongside the disciples to:
- **Show them** how to love God with their heart, soul, and mind
- **Teach them** what it looks like to follow God and live for him
- **Guide them** toward loving and serving others
- **Prepare them** to share the gospel and make disciples

Gosh, I love these examples from Jesus. These are ingredients that help us create an intentional pathway of discipleship for a teenage girl.

How do we make disciples with teenage girls?
We do it like Jesus did it. We follow his model.
We journey with girls the way he journeyed with the disciples.

We come alongside teenage girls to:
- **Show them** how to love Jesus and be loved by him
- **Teach them** to pursue Jesus
- **Guide them** toward loving and serving others
- **Prepare them** to GO and share the gospel

This is the way they become like Jesus.

This is the way we help them.

In a minute, we are going to unpack these four practices Jesus modeled for us. Before we do, I want to bring your attention to two little words I think can really impact the way we disciple.

PRACTICE AND EXPERIENCE
Let's look at these two words for a second.

Practice
When we want to excel at something, we practice. If we want to get better at a sport, learn a language, or perform a song, we practice. We practice so we can grow, expand our knowledge, succeed, thrive, and improve skills. When we practice, we create muscle memory, and when that happens, whatever we're working on has the potential to become second nature.

Now think of the word *practice* partnered up with our *faith*.

If we want to grow, thrive, improve our skills, and expand our thinking, we do that through practice. We practice things like prayer, silence and solitude, worship, and studying God's Word so those things become like second nature. We don't practice to "achieve," we practice to *grow*.

Disciplemaking with Girls

We practice the things of our faith because that practice results in more closeness with Jesus.

Jesus modeled the importance and power of practice.

He didn't just talk about the prayer with the disciples, they practiced.

Before he told them to spread the gospel to all nations, they practiced sharing it house to house.

Practice drew the disciples into more closeness with God.

Practice prepared the disciples for what Jesus asked them to do.

Practice led the disciples toward becoming like Jesus.

Experience

Think of a life-changing experience you've had. An encounter with someone, a faith milestone, a really good donut, or a moment with Holy Spirit. What do you remember? What was happening in that moment? What were you wearing or what song was playing or where were you? What made the experience life-changing?

It's amazing how an experience can transform thinking, redirect a path, soften a heart, change a life, or just stick for a lifetime.

Now think of the word *experience* partnered up with our *faith*.

Experiences create tangible moments and memories that cause concepts, disciplines, feelings, and convictions to root themselves in our heart, soul, and mind. When we experience things with Jesus, or we have experiences that are centered around him, it creates momentum in our relationship with him.

If you were to interview some of the girls I have discipled over the years, they would tell you that summer camp is hands down one of the most significant turning points in their relationship with Jesus. Why? Because it's an experience centered on him that creates momentum in their relationship with him and roots things out in their heart.

Becoming Like Jesus

Jesus gave the disciples tangible experiences with him.

He didn't just talk about the importance of caring for widows and orphans, they experienced it together.

They didn't just hear about God's provision, they experienced it through the multiplying of fishes and loaves.

They didn't just hear about the transforming life Jesus offered, they experienced it by watching a man pick up his mat and walk.

Experiences solidified and deepened belief for the disciples.

Experiences gave the disciples the opportunity to do things with Jesus before they did them on their own.

Experiences gave the disciples a picture of the mission before Jesus left them to carry it out.

Practice and experience are woven throughout Jesus's journey with the disciples, and they are things we can weave into our discipleship journey with teenage girls. Through practice and experience we can show, teach, guide, prepare, and encourage girls to become like Jesus.

Okay, now let's jump into those four practices of Jesus we were talking about a minute ago.

(Side note: Four is not the magic number. There are a variety of ways we can help teenage girls become like Jesus. Throughout the Gospels we see Jesus model many ways of nudging the disciples along. These are just four I am going to highlight, because good grief, we can't talk about them all. This book would be a thousand pages long.)

#1 SHOW GIRLS HOW TO LOVE JESUS AND BE LOVED BY HIM

Essential to being a disciple of Jesus is understanding how to love and be loved by him. It is easy to say, "I love you," but it takes intentionality and commitment to actually love and let yourself be loved. I find a lot of teenage girls come into the discipleship process with an initial love

Disciplemaking with Girls

for Jesus, but they don't understand what that means and how that forms and shapes us as believers. Part of becoming like him is growing a deeper understanding of the love that exists between us.

Loving Jesus
When Jesus says something is "the greatest" or the "most important," it's wise to pay attention.

Matthew 22:37-38 (NIV) says, "Jesus replied, 'You must love the LORD your God with all your heart, all your soul, and all your mind. **'This is the first and greatest commandment."**

Pay attention. The greatest thing we can do is love Jesus with everything we are. Our whole heart, mind, and soul. Again, it's easy to say "I love you, Jesus" but loving Jesus is a daily choice that requires commitment and action.

How do we help a teenage girl understand how to love Jesus?
Remind her: We love Jesus when we…

- are devoted to him (Definition of devotion: *love, loyalty, or enthusiasm for a person.*[20] This is a random side note. I just loved this thinking about this definition and our relationship with Jesus!)
- rely on him
- trust his plan for us and that he wants the very best for us
- are obedient to what he asks of us
- follow his lead in every area of our lives

Ways girls can practice this on their own or with a leader
Ways we can love Jesus:
- Worship him and praise him
- Baptism
- Show our gratitude to him
- Talk to him…a lot
- Love others in his name
- Identify as a child of God, understanding that who I am is based on whose I am, not the things that describe me

Becoming Like Jesus

- Honor him in the choices you make
- Let the fruit of the Spirit lead your attitude and actions
- Include him and make decisions that honor God's

Ways girls can experience this on their own or with a leader
Ways we can show our love to Jesus:

- Sing a worship song that praises Jesus's name out loud
- Tell Jesus five things we are grateful for every day
- Spend time with him in prayer
- Show compassion to a friend, a neighbor, or a family member in need
- Give generously of your time, gifts, and money
- Take communion and use it as a moment to reflect on what Jesus has done for you

Being loved by Jesus

I think this is a tough concept for teenage girls (and maybe humans in general). It easy to fall into the trap of believing you need to do something to earn Jesus's love. "If I do good things, if I am a good person, if I don't lie, cheat or steal, then Jesus will love me." But the truth is, Jesus just loves us. We don't have to do anything to earn it. He loves us at our best and at our worst. He loves us when we do good things, and he loves us just as much when we do bad things. We *get* to be loved by him, feel loved by him, and receive love from him without needing to be enough or do enough to deserve it.

1 John 4:19 (NIV) says, "We love because he first loved us." The tiny little verse contains such a powerful reminder. Jesus loved us first. Before we loved him. He knows love and he knows how to love us well.

How do we help a teenage girl understand how to allow herself to just be loved by Jesus?

Remind her: Jesus's love…

- is never-ending
- is unconditional
- runs deep

Disciplemaking with Girls

Ephesians 3: 18-19 (NLT) says,
> And may you have the power to understand, as all God's people should, how wide, how long, how high, and how deep his love is. May you experience the love of Christ, though it is too great to understand fully. Then you will be made complete with all the fullness of life and power that comes from God.

Jesus loves us and...
- nothing can separate us from his love.
- nothing in life or death can come between us and his love.
- no fear, worry, or power can weaken his love for us.

Romans 8:38-39 (NLT) says,

> And I am convinced that nothing can ever separate us from God's love. Neither death nor life, neither angels nor demons, neither our fears for today nor our worries about tomorrow— not even the powers of hell can separate us from God's love. No power in the sky above or in the earth below—indeed, nothing in all creation will ever be able to separate us from the love of God that is revealed in Christ Jesus our Lord.

Ways we can practice feeling loved by Jesus
- Spend time with him
- Think about or reflect on how much he loves us
- Read his words in Scripture
- Talk to him and listen for his voice

Ways we can experience Jesus's love for us
- Listen to a worship song or music centered on Jesus
- Hear a word of encouragement from one of God's people
- Spend time in nature experiencing his creation
- Read the book of John (There are many places in Scripture that highlight the love of Jesus. To me the book of John feels like a hug from Jesus. So many reminders and thoughts from him directly. Heart emoji!)

#2 TEACH THEM TO PURSUE JESUS

What do you think of when you think of the word "pursuit"? I think of a highway car chase. I am not sure what that says about me, but it is the first thing that popped into my mind. One car racing after another at extreme speeds. I realize this kind of car chase means something terrible is happening, but they are also very exciting to watch. I can only assume they are very exciting to be in as well.

Okay, focus. Jesus. Let's talk more about Jesus. Honestly, I do think there's some parallel between a high-speed pursuit coupled with our relationship with Jesus. Being in pursuit of Jesus is exciting and lovely and full of richness. We want teenage girls to understand that following Jesus is not the mundane Sunday drive—we want to them to connect with the idea that following him is a high-speed, action-packed, on-the-move kind of thing. It's chasing after Jesus in hopes of catching a stronger relationship with him, a greater knowledge of him, a more robust faith in him, and a deeper love for him.

A lot of teenage girls don't know how to do this. We need to teach them how to pursue Jesus. Oftentimes girls will follow the lead of others who are following Jesus but they have a harder time thinking of how to do this themselves.

- When a girl has big questions, how can we teach her to pursue Jesus's answers?
- How can we help a girl pursue different avenues of connection with him?
- When culture says something different from what God says, how do we help a girl pursue truth?
- When she needs encouragement, how do we teach her to seek Jesus in Scripture and prayer?

If we want girls to form habits of pursuit, we need to teach them how to do it.

Disciplemaking with Girls

How do we teach a teenage girl to pursue Jesus?

Teach her to GROW
Colossians 2:6-7 (NLT) says,

> And now, just as you accepted Christ Jesus as your Lord, you must continue to follow him. Let your roots grow down into him, and let your lives be built on him. Then your faith will grow strong in the truth you were taught, and you will overflow with thankfulness.

- Grow in her knowledge and understanding of God's character
- Grow in her knowledge and understanding of Jesus
- Grow in her knowledge and understanding of the Holy Spirit
- Grow in her understanding of the gospel
- Grow in her obedience, wisdom, and humility
- Grow in her understanding of truth

Teach her to SEEK
As Jesus says in Matthew 7:7-8 (NIV),

> "Ask and it will be given to you; seek and you will find; knock and the door will be opened to you. For everyone who asks receives; the one who seeks finds; and to the one who knocks, the door will be opened."

- Seek God for answers to big and small questions
- Seek his voice and his perspective
- Seek his wisdom and his opinion
- Seek reassurance and reminders of his love
- Seek holiness

Teach her to LEARN
As the psalmist writes in Psalm 86:11 (NLT),

Becoming Like Jesus

> Teach me your ways, O Lord, that I may live according to your truth!

- Learn to use her Bible (teach biblical literacy)
- Learn to incorporate spiritual disciplines into daily life
- Learn to use her spiritual gifts
- Learn to study Scripture and have an expanding knowledge of Scripture
- Learn to pray

Teach her to TRUST
As it says in Proverbs 3:5-6 (NLT),

> Trust in the Lord with all your heart; do not depend on your own understanding. Seek his will in all you do, and he will show you which path to take.

- Trust God's voice
- Trust Jesus
- Trust the Holy Spirit
- Trust in any circumstances

Teach her to UNDERSTAND
As it says in John 3:16-17 (NLT),

> For this is how God loved the world: He gave his one and only Son, so that everyone who believes in him will not perish but have eternal life. God sent his Son into the world not to judge the world, but to save the world through him.

- Jesus is in constant pursuit of her
- Jesus will never abandon her or give up his pursuit
- This is a two-way pursuit

How to practice this with a girl or group of girls
- Study one book of the Bible (looking at aspects like context, history, themes, characters, and application)

Disciplemaking with Girls

- Memorize a chapter or ten verses in the Bible
- Journal every day for a month
- Lead your group in Lectio Divina
- Sit in silence or solitude
- Ask Jesus your toughest question and listen for his response
- Look in Scripture for the answer to a big question you have
- Listen to God's voice and do what he tells you

How to experience this
- Interact with the Holy Spirit
- Interact with God
- Interact with Jesus
- Articulate the gospel to someone
- Go on a retreat with Jesus
- Find or designate a location for silence or solitude
- Take a spiritual gifts test or an assessment to discover gifts
- Engage in a worship experience
- Trust the Lord with something big that you have been holding back from doing

#3 GUIDE THEM TOWARD MINISTRY

Another essential to being a disciple is loving others the way Jesus loves others. Jesus talks about the second greatest commandment in Matthew 22. I know it's *second*, but Jesus says it is the SECOND MOST IMPORTANT THING—pretty important.

We find this commandment in Matthew 22:39-40 (NLT): "A second is equally important: 'Love your neighbor as yourself.' The entire law and all the demands of the prophets are based on these two commandments."

Jesus says the two most important things are to love God and love others. We've talked about helping girls love and live for God, so now let's tackle helping them love others.

Loving, serving, and putting others first are not the easiest things for a teenage girl. Remember way back in the beginning of the book when I talked about how egocentric they can be? Thinking about what they need or want first is the natural thought pattern of a teenage girl. Girls live in that "me" bubble. But in Matthew, Jesus asks us to adopt an unnatural way of thinking: to always look for ways to love and serve other people ahead of ourselves. We are most like Jesus when we are serving and loving others. The way we help teenage girls become like Jesus is to guide them toward "loving their neighbor" as much as they love themselves. NBD, am I right?

Guide a girl to love others

As John 13:34-35 (NLT) says, "So, now I am giving you a new commandment: Love each other. Just as I have loved you, you should love each other. Your love for one another will prove to the world that you are my disciples."

Well, that sums it up.

Our love for one another will show that we are disciples of Jesus.

Love others the way he loved us.

It's a love that includes acceptance, forgiveness, and compassion and is marked by selflessness and putting others first.

Becoming like Jesus means loving the way he does. So how do we guide a teenage girl to love others?

Ways girls can practice this on their own or with a leader

- Give genuine encouragement
- Earnestly pray for them
- Forgive and ask for forgiveness
- Show hospitality
- Share kind words
- Speak kindly of others, don't gossip, don't say hateful things about someone

Disciplemaking with Girls

- Show up and be present when someone is in need
- Grieve with, rejoice with, weep with, stand with others

Ways girls can experience this on their own or with a leader
- Write cards of encouragement to three people
- Choose one person to pray for and then pray with them
- Invite someone to eat a meal with you and pay for it
- Tell someone five things you love about them
- If you hear a rumor or gossip, don't spread it
- If you know someone is hurting, leave a note and treat on their doorstep reminding them of God's love
- Tell someone how much Jesus loves them
- Write thank you cards to teachers, coaches, parents, and any other adults who do cool things for you

Serve others

"Then a despised Samaritan came along, and when he saw the man, he felt compassion for him. Going over to him, the Samaritan soothed his wounds with olive oil and wine and bandaged them. Then he put the man on his own donkey and took him to an inn, where he took care of him. The next day he handed the innkeeper two silver coins, telling him, 'Take care of this man. If his bill runs higher than this, I'll pay you the next time I'm here.'

Now which of these three would you say was a neighbor to the man who was attacked by bandits?" Jesus asked. The man replied, "The one who showed him mercy." Then Jesus said, "Yes, now go and do the same." — Luke 10:33-37 (NLT)

Jesus tells us to "go and do the same."

Who is our neighbor? Everyone is our neighbor. This is not just about the street we live on or the community we live in. Every person is our neighbor, and he calls us to serve them with compassion, mercy, and generosity.

Becoming Like Jesus

Ways girls can practice this on their own or with a leader
- Pray for God to give you opportunities to serve others
- Don't think someone else is going to do it, jump in
- Start each day by asking God to open your eyes to the needs around you
- When someone asks for help, say yes
- Use your gifts and abilities
- Show compassion, empathy, and mercy

Ways girls can experience this on their own or with a leader
- Share your lunch with someone who doesn't have one
- Sit with someone who is sitting alone (and doesn't want to)
- Serve in a ministry at the church
- Hold the door for someone
- Do a household chore without being asked
- Cook dinner for your family, a friend, or a neighbor
- Serve in your community
- Donate your money to something worthwhile
- Clean out your closet and share with a friend or a local homeless shelter
- Do something kind for a teacher at school without being asked

#4 PREPARE THEM TO GO AND SHARE THE GOSPEL

Every moment Jesus spent with his disciples was about preparing them for the future mission.

As it says in Matthew 28:19-20 (NLT),

> Jesus came and told his disciples, "I have been given all authority in heaven and on earth. Therefore, go and make disciples of all the nations, baptizing them in the name of the Father and the Son and the Holy Spirit. Teach these new disciples to obey all the commands I have given you. And be sure of this: I am with you always, even to the end of the age."

Disciplemaking with Girls

His final words were a call to action. I've often tried to imagine what the disciples were feeling in this moment. Were they excited? Were they shaking in their boots? Did they feel equipped? Did they know where to begin? How long after Jesus ascended did they stand there? I imagine they felt a mix of many things. Some nervousness and insecurity partnered with excitement and empowerment. But no matter what they were feeling, Jesus had been preparing them to share the good news and to GO.

Every disciple is called by Jesus to make disciples. This is an essential part of becoming like him. Christ wants all of us to tell others about his love and the difference he can make in their lives.

I think this can be intimidating for teenage girls. In today's world, you don't know how someone might respond and that unknown feels a little scary. Teenage girls don't love being rejected. This call to action from Jesus isn't the easiest one to lean into. And even though they are being asked to share the best news ever, it requires vulnerability, courage, and humility—three more things that can be a little tough for a teenage girl.

So, how can we prepare girls to respond to this call to action and go make disciples?

Prepare a girl to go and share the gospel

There are three ways we as leaders and youth workers can help make this less intimidating. Notice I said *less*. I am not sure any amount of preparation will remove all scary feelings and insecurities, but I do think preparing in these ways can instill confidence and excitement.

1. Invite girls into making disciples.

Helping our girls get more comfortable with the idea of making disciples requires a little vision casting. Jesus did a great job casting vision in the Great Commission, so this is not a "recast," but more of an invitation to them to be part of something amazing.

One of the verses I use often to invite girls into disciplemaking is 1 Thessalonians 2:8 (NLT). It says, "We loved you so much that we shared with you not only God's Good News but our own lives, too."

Becoming Like Jesus

I love this verse. It's the perfect picture of what we want to prepare girls to do.

This verse says…

…because we love you so much…
…we shared the good news with you…
…and we shared our lives with you.

This is how we are making disciples with girls. Sharing life, loving them well through relationships, and sharing Jesus with them. Let's invite girls into this kind of disciplemaking.

2. Prepare them to share the gospel

The word "gospel" means "good news" because that's exactly what it is. But there are a lot of teenage girls who have a difficult time articulating what the good news is. We want them to understand the meaning of the gospel in their own lives first, so you might need to pause this part of disciple training and spend time on that before you do anything else. Once they have an understanding and knowledge of how the gospel transforms their own life, THEN get on with the preparation for them to share it with other people.

The more prepared they feel, the more confident they will be to share.

3. Prepare them to share their story with Jesus

One of the ways we can open a conversation about the gospel is by sharing about the life change we experienced through our story with Jesus. We can prepare a girl to go and make disciples by helping her craft her testimony—her story with Jesus. Stories of life change are powerful, so helping a girl craft and share hers might just lead someone to Jesus.

How do we prepare a teenage girl to go and share the gospel?

Help girls share the story of Jesus

Help girls *practice* sharing the gospel out loud.

Walk through Romans together and utilize the Scripture pathway to

Disciplemaking with Girls

discover and shape something for them to share.
Romans 3:23, Romans 6:23, Romans 5:8, Romans 10:9
I love Romans 10:13-14 (NLT) as an inspiration in this area:

> For everyone who calls on the name of the Lord will be saved. But how can they call on Him to save them unless they believe in Him? And how can they believe in Him if they have never heard about Him? And how can they hear about Him unless someone tells them?

Have a conversation with girls around this passage that helps you jump into practice.

Help girls share their story
Help girls craft their testimony, and help them *practice* sharing their story with Jesus out loud.

"Testimony" is just a fancy way of saying "your story of life with Jesus." Creating and sharing a testimony gives the opportunity to reflect on your life and recognize how Jesus has impacted, directed, and blessed you. Sharing your testimony is one of the best ways to tell others about Jesus and the life-changing power he can have on their lives.

Prompts to guide girls as they shape or create the story:
1. What were your attitudes and actions like before you became a Christian?
2. How have your attitudes and actions changed since you became a Christian?
3. Talk about some significant moments in your walk with Christ.
4. Talk about what life with Jesus is like.

Help girls experience this
Help a girl choose someone with whom to share her story and the gospel.
- **PRAY** for a friend and choose a time and date to share your story and share the story of Jesus.

Becoming Like Jesus

- Does this friend know you're a Christian? The first step is to let them know before you share. How can you **TELL** your friend you love Jesus?
- **SHARE** your story and the gospel on the time and day you committed to.
- If an opportunity arises to pray with your friend to receive Jesus, then you are empowered to **LEAD** them.

LAST THOUGHTS

The content in this chapter doesn't make up a series of steps to follow. This is not a linear pathway.

These four areas are not meant feel like a discipleship checklist. They are really just four essential parts of a disciple that you focus on depending on where a girl is in her journey with Jesus. While we want to be intentional in the way we journey with girls, disciplemaking doesn't necessarily follow a specific, orderly path. Jesus was all over the place with the disciples. One minute he was teaching, then he was throwing them into ministry, and then they were retreating to pray. The same will be true for you and the girls you disciple. You will find yourself jumping around as opportunities arise.

Remember, this is a process.

When you begin discipling girls, it's natural to want the discipleship to move along and grow steadily. But every girl's journey with Jesus is different and moves at a different pace. The process of becoming like Jesus is just that: a process. You are walking with girls over time. So, try to release any expectations of how discipleship "should" go with the girls entrusted to you. Relax and be reassured that whatever pace or path you find yourself on, it's the right one.

Chapter Twelve:
Partnership with Parents

PARENTS ARE A VITAL PART OF THE DISCIPLESHIP PROCESS
I end my small group every week with a time of prayer. I know, that's some crazy cutting-edge stuff. When we have about fifteen minutes left in group, we close out what we're doing and open it up for prayer requests. It's always a mixed bag of focus and tangents, and every girl has a different comfort level with sharing and praying. I love prayer as the last thing we do together before they leave.

One Wednesday night, Emily raised her hand just before we opened the floor for requests. She asked, "Can I share an idea for our prayer time?" I said, "Absolutely!" (I was a little too enthusiastic in my response, but I get really excited when a student wants to do something out of the norm.) Emily explained her idea to the group. "Everyone go around and share one word that describes how you are feeling today and the name of one person you want us to pray for. Then, we will pray for both." She looked at me with questioning eyes, and I responded with a head nod and told her I thought it was a great idea.

It was the first time that everyone in our group shared. Girls were saying words like "overwhelmed," "anxious," "grateful," "tired," and even "hungry." Then they shared names like Mom, Dad, sibling, coach, teacher, and friend. We prayed over the words and the names and it ended up being a really powerful time. After group, I asked Emily how she came up with that idea. She kind of put her head down and mumbled something under her breath. So, I asked again. "How did you come up with that?" She had a kind of bashful look on her face as she said, "It was my mom's idea." I couldn't tell if she was embarrassed or just feeling shy about it. She said, "At night when my mom comes in to

Disciplemaking with Girls

say goodnight, she asks me to share one word that describes how I am feeling and the name of one person she can pray for. And then we pray together."

Cue the lump in my throat visualizing a mom and daughter experiencing the prayer time I'd just had with my small group. "Wow, Emily, I think it is really cool that you and your mom pray together. I loved that prayer idea and I think we should do more often in our group. What do you think?"

She looked at me, smiled really big, and nodded her head. When her mom came to pick her up, I told her about the group prayer time and Emily's suggestion. She smiled and her eyes welled up a bit. She said, "I started doing that because she is so reserved and keeps so much inside. When I would ask her how I could pray for her, it seemed like she would tense up and was too overwhelmed to share. So, I started just asking for one word and one person to try lessening the pressure. It's become my favorite time of the day. Sitting at the end of her bed and praying together. She also asks me what my two words are and she prays for me now. It's really cool."

Cue lump number two in my throat. I thought my heart was going to explode. "Wow, that is amazing," I said. "I love the way you are loving and leading your daughter. You modeled something for her that then encouraged and influenced a bunch of girls tonight. So, thank you, and great job."

We use that prayer practice in our group almost every week now.

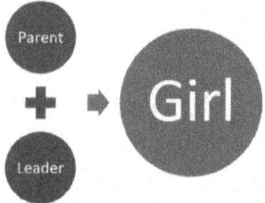

Parents' influence in the life of a teenage girl is undeniable. Nothing comes close to the consistent time and space they occupy together. They do more life with their daughter than anyone else, so there truly is no one better to consistently point her to Jesus. A girl might not admit that her parents have influence in her life, but they do.

Emily was a little bashful to admit her mom's role in the prayer moment, but that didn't make it any less impactful. Her mom was practicing prayer with her nightly and that took root in Emily's heart, so much so that she brought it to her small group of friends.

Girls need a bunch of people besides their parents at the discipleship table with them, but they also *really need* their parents. It is the partnership between parents and caring adults that makes the biggest impact on a girl's life.

When I think of that partnership I picture an Olympic track. I like to think of girls, caring adults, and parents running on the track together. We are all running in the same direction, toward the same finish line, but in our separate lanes. We all play our distinct roles in the discipleship journey, but we are hopefully running toward the same result.

To be transparent for a second, I did not always understand the importance of this partnership. This was even once I'd become a parent myself. I thought my role as the youth pastor was the most important in helping a kid become a disciple of Jesus. I thought the partnership with parents was based on calendar, communication, and conflict. (I didn't mean for all of those to start with C, but here we are.) The truth is, for the first chunk of my ministry career, I felt mostly frustration with parents. I had thoughts like, "Why don't you pick up your kid on time?" or "Why are you sending me a two-page email single spaced about how disappointed you are?" or "I am sorry you're upset that camp sold out and your kid does not have a spot, even though the registration has been open for four months." My ministry to parents seemed to rally around solving problems and soothing frustrations. In many ways, I felt like it was me *vs.* parents. I didn't understand why they couldn't just get on board with what I was doing. And I certainly didn't take any time to understand where they were coming from or what their role was in the discipleship of their kid.

Thankfully, I recognized the error of my ways and learned how valuable our partnership could be. Parents and youth workers/volunteers truly are meant to work in tandem with teenage girls and there is a place for both roles in their discipleship.

The role of a parent in disciplemaking is vital.

The role of other caring adults in disciplemaking is vital.

Our shared role is working together to help a teenage girl become like Jesus.

PROFILE OF A PARENT
Who is the parent?
I realize the statement, "Parents play a vital role" raises all sorts of questions:

- What if there is no parent(s)?
- What if the parent doesn't love Jesus?
- What if the parent isn't connected to a faith community?
- What if a parent doesn't want to play a role in the discipleship process?
- What if one parent loves Jesus and the other doesn't?

I don't have answers to all the questions, but I do know that a large percentage of girls have a consistent caregiver. Homes today are filled with different types of families. Some are multigenerational, some are foster homes, some have a blended family dynamic, some have single parents, and some are traditional old two-parent households. For our purposes in the rest of this chapter, I am going to use "parents" as the term to represent all of the scenarios and family makeups listed above (and all of the many possibilities I didn't list). Regardless of the exact family structure, girls become stronger disciples when parents and caring adults are partnered up.

This parent/caring adult partnership might need to look different from girl to girl based on the parent's level of spiritual maturity, involvement in a faith community, or desire to participate. Still, I believe partnerships with different levels of expectations can be established and can all contribute to a girl's relationship with Jesus.

Partnership with Parents

For example: How should a youth worker or volunteer approach partnership with a parent who isn't connected to your faith community or doesn't love Jesus?

- Make a good first impression, be kind, and begin building a relationship.
- Communicate purpose, vision, and programs so they understand what you are doing in your ministry, small group, etc.
- Provide clear communication about expectations of their daughter, costs, and time commitments.
- Avoid using insider language.

Partnering starts with building relationships. No matter the scenario with a parent, there are always opportunities to connect, build a relationship, and partner in caring for a girl. Again, the level of that partnership might look different, but working together is the ultimate goal. It's also true that where you begin with a parent might not be where you end up. No matter where you start there are many possibilities ahead.

Understanding parents

What makes a parent tick? Parents are real people with thoughts and feelings (sometimes a lot of feelings). Understanding parents better can help us build stronger partnerships with them.

MYTHS ABOUT PARENTS	TRUTH ABOUT PARENTS
They are working out of a handbook that taught them to parent perfectly	Just as every student is unique, so is every parent
They understand their teenager	It's highly likely they are doing the best they can with what they've got
They have it all together because they are grown-ups	You CAN minister to parents if you are NOT a parent of a teenager
They remember everything you say and read all of your emails/texts in their entirety	You can empathize with parents on a different level if you ARE a parent of a teenager
They don't need encouragement	Every parent needs encouragement, prayer, help, and hope

Put yourself in a parent's shoes: What is likely on a parent's mind?

- The stats about today's teenagers feel dismal and overwhelming

Disciplemaking with Girls

- Technology is advancing faster than parents can track
- Parents are constantly comparing themselves with other parents (often via social media)
- The generational differences are more glaring than in generations past
- The church is viewed as _____ (fill in the blank with however it's viewed in your community or context)
- Parents themselves are figuring out what their own faith looks like in today's culture
- The COVID-19 pandemic: I don't know what else to say about this other than it was a thing for parents

Every parent wants their daughter to…
- be happy
- be liked/have friends
- genuinely be less lonely
- feel accepted and seen
- be healthy (emotionally, mentally, physically, relationally)

Most Christian parents want their daughter to have…
- a worldview
- success in the things they attempt
- a future as a functioning adult
- a love or a like for the church
- a growing relationship with Jesus
- a developing faith that leads into adulthood

Taking time to think about parents and understanding who they are leads to stronger partnerships. It also grows our empathy for them, it grows the grace we extend to them, and it brings a thoughtfulness to our approach that will help us to be more effective in our journey to disciple girls.

Helping parents understand
Just as it's important that we build our perspective of who parents are,

Partnership with Parents

there are also some things it's important we help parents understand. Some parents know exactly how to play their role in the partnership with a youth worker or adult leader, but some don't.

Help parents understand their discipleship role
Think back to the job description chapter. We talked about the fact that leaders can be at their most effective when they understand what to do. The same is true for parents: If we want them to win in their role, we need to give them a picture of what it is. The parents you work with are likely coming from many perspectives and backgrounds. Regardless of their potential differences, here are a few things to communicate to parents that will give them a more robust understanding of discipling their teenage daughter.

Tell parents...
- No matter what your daughter thinks, or what her facial expression tells you, you are one of the most influential people in her life. Maybe even *the most* influential.
- You spend more time with your daughter than anyone else. There truly is no one better than you to consistently point your her to Jesus.
- As a Christ-follower*, you are called to make disciples, and your daughter is included in that. A disciplemaker is a dedicated disciple of Jesus who is striving to lead by example, live with integrity, and is committed to pass down the ways of Jesus to the next generation. (*Don't say this to a parent who doesn't love Jesus, but you could use this to explain your role to them.)
- Since your role is to make disciples, the definition of disciple we'll use is *a dedicated follower of Jesus who is striving to learn from him, stay close with him, and be led by him in daily life.*
- Practice following Jesus together with your daughter through worship, serving, participating in the church body, studying God's Word, prayer, fun, conversation, and consistency.
- Talk with other parents of teenage girls so you feel normal about what is happening with yours and gain ideas from how others are doing it.
- You are not alone in this. Ask for help when you need it because

every parent needs it.
- This is a process. You are putting your daughter on a trajectory for lifelong faith. Faith development happens over time. Take a deep breath and submit to God's pace.

Help parents understand their daughter

I don't know of a greater ministry to parents than helping them understand more about their teenage daughter. If you can give parents even the tiniest insight into why their girl is the way she is, I can see gifts and weeping from parents in your future. It's important for us as youth workers to understand our girls, and we absolutely want the same for parents. The more each of us understands about teenage girls, the more effective and thoughtful we can be in the disciplemaking process.

I encourage you to break down the first few chapters of this book and share those insights with parents. This is just a starting point, but again, *anything* we pass on to parents is going to be helpful.

You can also…
- Send parents the most up-to-date research about the current generation
- Point them to podcasts, blogs, books, and articles that highlight learnings about teenage girls
- Encourage parents to spend unstructured time with their daughter and process what they observe
- Tell parents to get coffee with their daughter's small group leader, teacher, or coach

Help parents understand the youth ministry

It's easy to assume all parents know who you are and what your youth ministry is about, but that is not always the case. Communicating basics about the purpose of your youth ministry and how you intend to partner with them gives parents clear expectations of the church's role in the discipleship. Questions to answer for parents about your youth ministry:
1. Why does your youth ministry exist?

Partnership with Parents

2. What is the goal for every student who participates?
3. What can parents expect from your partnership with them?

I suggest creating a one-page document or a digital graphic that you can easily distribute to parents. I also think it is wise to think about communication, care, and church involvement.

Communication
The goal is good two-way communication between the youth ministry team and parents. Clear, concise communication is something most parents value. Questions to ask yourself to grow in this area:
- How do you communicate to parents inside your church and outside your church? How often do you communicate?
- What are your avenues of communication to parents? Website, text, social platforms, email?
- What do parents need to know?

Care
When youth ministries offer care for girls who are struggling, hurting, or in need of help, it can operate as a front door for your youth ministry*. Ask yourself what kind of care structure you have in place. If you have more than three girls in your youth ministry, this is a worthwhile area to think through. Questions to ask yourself about your ministry and then communicate to parents:
- Who can parents contact if their daughter needs care?
- What resources are available in the church and in the community?
- Who is available to meet with girls and/or their parents?

With double the number of girls as boys struggling with mental health (according to the CDC), I am being serious when I say this is a front door to faith for a teenage girl.

Church involvement
How does a girl get involved in your youth ministry? Think through your answers to the following questions and then communicate them to parents:
- How does she build relationships?

Disciplemaking with Girls

- What are the most important areas for her to get involved with?
- How does she grow in her relationship with Jesus?
- How does she get involved in ministry or serving?

Parents don't need to know everything about your ministry, they just need to understand the basics. Don't overcomplicate it, don't use insider language, and give clear onramps to involvement.

ENCOURAGE PARENTS TO MAKE DISCIPLES
Starting points for discipleship

A few years ago, I was leading a training for parents at my church. The audience was made up of parents of sixth to twelfth grade students. When I talked with them, I shared a lot of the things we have covered so far in this chapter. I told them they are the most influential person in their student's life, that we are meant to partner in helping make disciples, and I unpacked what the parents' role could be in that. I was feeling pretty good about the meeting and the content. There was a good turnout and there were lots of nods and smiles while I was talking.

After the meeting, though, I had an interesting debrief conversation with Lindsey's mom. She walked up to me looking a little dazed. I asked how she was doing, and she responded with, "I don't know." I asked if there was something I could clarify? "Um, all of it. I have no idea what I'm supposed to do." Panic started to creep into her voice; she was clearly feeling really overwhelmed. She said, "I thought you were going to disciple my daughter. I mean, I have no idea what to do. I am not a pastor. I don't know that much about the Bible. I have no idea how to disciple my daughter."

I put my hand on her arm and told her to take a deep breath. I told her we are in it together and we would take it one step at a time. I also told her I had a few resources that could give her some starting points for helping her daughter grow closer to Jesus.

What I realized in that moment is that every parent has a different comfort level with this role of disciplemaker. I had pitched it to parents as this exciting thing that they get to be a part of in their daughter's life, but for some that was paralyzing and terrifying. I don't think Lindsey's mom was actually incapable of this role; I think she just needed a few starting points. I had given a job description to parents without telling them where to begin or how to do it. For some parents, disciplemaking is intuitive and a lot of guidance is not necessary, but there are more than a few out there who might appreciate some direction.

Below are four different starting points I gave to Lindsey's mom.

Starting point #1: follow Jesus in front of your daughter
Let go of any pressure you feel to have it all together or live out a perfect faith in front of your daughter. First, it's not possible, and second, it doesn't help her. Following Jesus in front of your daughter will help her understand that you are still on the journey, just like she is. She needs you to be authentic, showing her the wonderful pieces of following Jesus and the places where it is tough. You can model authenticity through your vulnerability, humility, and honesty about your relationship with Jesus. Teenage girls will catch so much just by watching you live for Jesus. Share your real prayer requests with them, be generous to others in front of them, and sing worship songs at the top of your lungs in the car in front of them. Be a disciple as you help her become a disciple.

Idea: Share your testimony
Does your teen know about your journey with Jesus? Does she know where and how it began? The ups and downs you have experienced in your faith journey? Or what your relationship with Jesus looks like today? It is important for your teen girl to hear your story with Jesus because your life is proof of his redeeming power. Knowing how Jesus saved and changed you can help your student have greater faith in Jesus and give her hope for her own salvation and sanctification.

At the same time, sharing where it has been difficult for you gives your daughter the freedom to share about her own doubts and the tough spots in her faith. I know it can be intimidating as a parent to be vulnerable and open up to our kids, but this can be an amazing way for you and your daughter to connect. Begin praying ahead of time for God to open a window to share your story!

Prayerfully reflect and write out your testimony before sharing with your student.

Disciplemaking with Girls

Your testimony could include:
- Your life before Jesus (use discernment)
- How Jesus revealed your sin and his grace to you
- How your life has changed through the power of Christ
- Moments of God's goodness and faithfulness
- Moments of doubts or questions

Starting point #2: initiate a faith conversation

There are all sorts of conversations you initiate daily with your daughter. Just as it is important to ask how her day was, it is also important to ask how she is doing in her walk with Jesus. It is valuable to normalize and create safe spaces for faith conversations. You want your daughter to understand that you are a safe person to share and express what she is thinking about, processing through, and questioning in her faith journey.

Some of the prompts parents can use to initiate a conversation:
- Tell me about your relationship with Jesus right now?
- What have you been learning about at church or small group?
- What big questions are you asking God right now?
- Do you have a favorite Bible verse or book of the Bible right now?
- What are a few things you are grateful to God for right now?
- How can I be praying for you?
- How can I be praying for your friends?

Starting point #3: do fun things together

It might seem weird that "have fun" is a priority in strengthening your daughter as a disciple. But as we looked at earlier, fun leads to trust and trust leads to depth and it's in the depth where disciplemaking happens. Building trust opens the door to meaningful conversations about Jesus. Sometimes you need a few fun memories, experiences, and inside jokes to get you to that place with your daughter. Fun with your kid is never a waste of time. It's often through these fun moments that we are launched into some of the best conversations about a life lived with and for Jesus.

Partnership with Parents

Four fun outings to build deeper relationships with your daughter:

- *Late Start or Ditch Day*
  We are advocates for education in student ministry. Every once in a while, though, it can be really refreshing to toss your daughter's normal routine out the window. Plan a "late start breakfast" and go a little late to school, or plan a "ditch day" and skip the whole day all together! Not all teenagers like surprises, so you will need to be cautious about how you spring the news of the time off. And make sure there is nothing major happening academically or socially on the day you choose. Times like these can be life-giving and life-changing for your relationship with your daughter. It is something they will always remember. And in the grand timeline of their life, missing a little school is not going to affect whether or not they become the president.

- *Movie Night*
  Sometimes it is just about being together and not talking. Find a movie you can both attend and sit side by side. Eat snacks and watch the movie. It might not feel like meaningful time, but non-verbal fun and communication can be just as powerful as verbal communication. And, depending on whether the movie is good or bad you will have a great conversation on the way home!

- *Twenty Questions*
  Take a jar or a bucket or an envelope and fill it with twenty questions on separate strips of paper. Go to a favorite treat spot and go back and forth asking the questions. Your daughter's likes and dislikes change often, so you could use the same questions multiple times. One of the ways girls feel affirmed is by being known. Make it your mission to "know" the little things about them and then use that information to affirm them throughout the week.

- *"Would You Rather?" Day*
  Most of the time, our girls are on someone else's agenda. What if for one day they got to make all the choices? Create some different options, but give them the freedom to make the final choices! Some ideas:

  Would you rather....lunch (Taco Bell or picnic)
  Would you rather....fun activity (mini golf or bowling)
  Would you rather...coffee or dessert (Starbucks or ice cream)

Disciplemaking with Girls

Starting point #4: Weekly family devotion
Choose a day of the week when you and your daughter can spend some time worshipping together. Set aside time to pray, sing, and read God's Word.

Consider choosing the same day and time each week. Consistency could help it become something both of you really look forward to!

Suggestions for this time:
- Open with prayer
- Sing or listen to a worship song together
- Read a Bible passage together (maybe go through a book of the Bible)
- Share thoughts, questions, or learnings about the passage with each other
- Share prayer requests and pray *with* one another

BUILDING A MINISTRY TO PARENTS
In youth ministry, there is typically a long list of priorities. I mentioned before that parents used to be at the bottom of my list, but over the years my mindset has shifted greatly. While my primary ministry is focused on teenagers, I now understand that God is also using me in the lives of their parents. I have weekly opportunities to partner with parents in the discipleship of their daughters, but I also have the opportunity to *minister to parents* as well. So, what are some ways we can build a parent ministry that includes partnership and care?

Start with questions
A good place to begin building a parent ministry is to evaluate your current ministry to parents. Questions are always a great place to begin, and listening to the answers will help you kickstart new strategies.

Reflection questions
- Do I have a strategy and structure for parent ministry?
- Do I have relationships with parents in my ministry?
- What kind of time in my week do I dedicate to parents?
- What kind of resources do I have available for parents?

Partnership with Parents

- Where do I point parents when they need help?
- How am I encouraging/helping parents to disciple their students?
- How do I communicate what is available for parents?
- How do I communicate with parents?
- How do I currently care for hurting parents?
- Do parents feel comfortable sharing a concern with me? Do they know they can? Who do they call when they have a concern?

Create a strategy
Allow the answers to these questions to inform and create a basic framework for the parent ministry you want to build. It does not need to be complicated, it just needs to be thoughtful. On the next page is a sample of the parent strategy at my church. It's not the most "cutting edge" approach, but it gives us the focus we need to partner and care for parents well.

Choose to do a few things well
A little goes a long way in parent ministry. I have found that doing two or three things really well tends to make the biggest impact while also helping me balance my time. As you build a parent ministry, keep in mind that it won't require a forty-point plan to be effective. Your parent ministry just needs to be thoughtful, promoting disciplemaking with teenage girls and providing care for parents who need it. You can be safe place for teenage girls *and their parents.*

Train small group leaders or other adults in your ministry to value partnership with parents
As we build our team of disciplemakers, we want to equip them to partner with the parents of the girls who have been entrusted to them.

Sample Small Group Leader Training: Partnering with Parents

The role of caring adults in disciplemaking is vital. Our *combined role* means PARTNERING together to help a teenage girl become like Jesus. As a leader in our ministry, it's important to understand the priority of parent involvement in spiritual development, as well as the opportunity to minister to parents weekly.

UNDERSTAND WHAT PARENTS VALUE
- They value togetherness
- They value impact
- They value flexibility and choices

MAKE A PERSONAL CONNECTION
- Be excited to see parents (their teenagers rarely are!)
- Learn names, and make an effort to remember stories and follow up
- Pray for your families

Side note: You might be the front door or first invitation to church

THINK "US + PARENTS" RATHER THAN "US VS. PARENTS"
- Be a fan in front of students
- Be a fan in front of parents
- Look for ways to include parents in what you are doing

GIVE THEM DISCIPLESHIP STARTING POINTS
- Offer parents conversation starters, Scripture, and memory makers

OFFER HOPE & HELP
- Listen and encourage
- Know what is available and point them to resources

CLEAR COMMUNICATION
- Clear communication builds trust
- Communicate with parents through multiple avenues (email, text, etc.). Plan events ahead of time and give parents detailed information about your plans[21]

Partnership with Parents

LAST THOUGHTS

As the mom of two daughters, I am truly grateful for the caring adults who have come alongside my husband, Ron, and me in the discipleship of our girls. We've had a village of other adult voices speaking into them, all playing different roles in the disciplemaking process. My girls had incredible small group leaders who consistently showed up and pointed them to Jesus. When Ron and I hit rough moments as parents, these were the people we called. When Ella and her boyfriend broke up, we called Emma, her small group leader, to come over and help us nurse her broken heart. When Abby was anxious about choosing a college, we called Roccio, her small group leader, to pray with us. When Ella hit a dark time at the end of her senior year, we rallied Audrey, Megan, Patti, Matt, Bryce, Kailey, and Emma around her in prayer. The partnership with these people has meant everything to us as parents. It has been such a life-giving experience to know we are not alone as we try our best to point our girls to Jesus.

Ella and Abby are now twenty-two and nineteen and they love Jesus. They are still growing and figuring out various pieces of their faith, but they are walking with him and they are actively involved in a community of believers. I believe it was the partnership between us and those small group leaders that led to where they are now. I am teary as I write this. I feel such deep gratitude.

I know everyone's experience is not exactly like ours. But I share this with you because I want to highlight the partnership. I would like to believe that I would have the same level of gratitude whether my girls were now walking with Jesus or not. The partnership with other adults was a source of strength and support and care and love for our whole family.

Our son is entering middle school next year and our prayer has been for God to send us new partners. I am emotional thinking about his journey ahead. And I am hopeful that in our partnership with caring adults who love Jesus, our son will also become a devoted disciple of Jesus. More than anything, though, I feel a little more relaxed knowing we don't have to go it alone.

Investing in this partnership with parents is worth your time.

Parents need this partnership, and they need you.

We are both vital to the discipleship process. Our girls need a strong village around them showing up consistently and pointing them to Jesus.

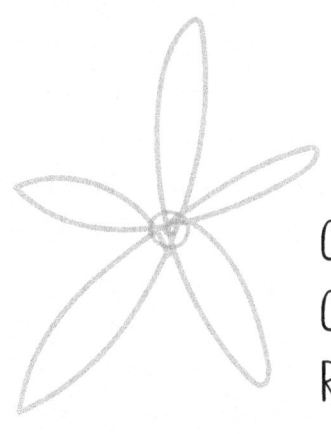

Chapter Thirteen:
Creating Rallying Points for
Relational Discipleship

I love romantic comedies. It's my favorite movie genre. Honestly, I love all cheesy movies. I am sucker for joyfulness and warmth and happily ever afters. And don't get me started on channels committed to cheesy Christmas movies—my heart could literally explode watching those. But I *really* love romcoms.

One of the things I love is the moment when the two main characters meet. In the movies this is called a "meet-cute." Oxford defines a meet-cute as *an amusing or charming first encounter between two characters that leads to the development of a romantic relationship between them.*[22]

The meet-cute is one of my favorite moments because it is the launching point for the whole movie. There is something magical about watching the genesis of a relationship. Because really, every relationship begins somewhere. Maybe not with a meet-cute situation, but there is always some sort of unique crossroads that brings people together.

Think of some of the most significant people in your life. Think about when, where, and how you met. Did you bump into each other randomly? Were you on the same team? Did you meet at work, or sit next to each other at church? Did someone introduce you or did you find yourselves together at an awkward birthday party?

I met my very best friend at a vending machine. We worked in the same office, and every day at 4 p.m. we each would walk to the vending machine to buy candy. We hit our afternoon slump at the same time, so we would chat at the vending machine almost every day. One afternoon she asked me to go to lunch and we've been besties ever since.

Disciplemaking with Girls

Twenty-five years of friendship because we both craved late afternoon chocolate.

All relationships have a genesis, including discipleship relationships. I am not suggesting that we try to arrange meet-cutes between leaders and girls, but I do know disciplemaking relationships need to start somewhere. They need intentional spaces designed to connect and then launch them into the discipleship process.

We spent the last chapter unpacking the "what" of disciplemaking, and now we need to spend some time unpacking "how" and "where" it happens. What does it look like to create spaces for discipleship relationships to begin and grow?

Where are the spaces we show, teach, guide, and empower teenage girls in their relationship with Jesus? And where are the places we practice and experience being followers of Jesus?

There are many ways to answer these questions, but relational discipleship will always need a rallying point where leaders and girls can meet. I want to highlight three potential launching pads for disciplemakers and disciples. These are pretty general, but that's intentional. I realize everyone reading this is coming from a different context and different circumstances, so I want to give you things to think about vs. specific plans. This is more about creating opportunities to launch relationships than it is about building a program.

For each launching pad, I am going to share two parts:

Environment: the physical space we create that sets the stage for relational discipleship to happen.

Elements: the intentional pieces of program that point a girl toward becoming a stronger disciple. Emphasize opportunities to *show, teach, guide, and empower.*

LAUNCHING PAD #1: BIG GROUPS
Okay: before we go any further, do not get caught up on the word "big." I am not talking about a certain number here. If you have a youth

Creating Rallying Points for Relational Discipleship

group of fifteen, the big group would be when all fifteen are gathered. If you have a classroom of twenty-five, the big group would be when all twenty-five are together. If you are at a summer camp of 100, the big group would be when all 100 are in the same session. An example of where we see "big group" disciplemaking is when Jesus teaches the Sermon on the Mount. As it says in Matthew 5:1-2 (NIV), "Now when Jesus saw the crowds, he went up on a mountainside and sat down. His disciples came to him, and he began to teach them." It might seem to be counterintuitive based on what we've talked about up until this point, but big group discipleship can work. In this big group, Jesus is with the disciples, he's modeling ministry, and he's teaching. This is relational discipleship in a big group. Are you with me?

Environment
- Outdoors, indoors, classroom, gym, or large closet
- Warm, inviting, colorful, and bright
- Safe space where a girl can be herself
- Music playing that sets the stage for discipleship
- Comfortable places to sit and build relationships
- The space is thoughtfully set up for the teenagers occupying it
- Designated leaders are ready to receive girls in the space, prepared to encourage, welcome, and learn names, and equipped for relational discipleship

Elements
- **Fun:** games, icebreakers, or videos that help build relationships and deepen trust. Laughing, smiling, and having fun together help teenagers relax and connect with other elements in the program.
- **Teaching moments:** sermon, message, communication, or teaching video. Something that gives teenagers the opportunity to learn, grow, discover, explore, and experience God's Word together.
- **Connect points:** intentional moments for leaders and teenagers to connect.
- **Guide:** encourage girls toward a next step or a way for teens to grow in their relationship with Jesus.
- **Practice:** musical worship, communion, prayer, studying God's

Disciplemaking with Girls

Word, or serving (there are so many things the big group can practice together).

Questions to get you thinking
- How will teenage girls connect with a leader in this space?
- How can a girl deepen her relationship with Jesus in this space?
- How will you connect and communicate with parents about this space?
- What resources will you need?

Example
Sydney attends our 11:00 Sunday morning church service for high school students. It is a space for guys and girls, and about seventy-five students attend weekly. It has many of the elements I listed above: It is a "big group" space. Every week I see Sydney and we have a conversation about her poetry, her animé artwork, and her relationship with Jesus. We spend an equal amount of time talking about all of these areas. When I met Syd, she was eleven and she did not know Jesus. She was a middle school wallflower and for the first year of our relationship, I did most of the talking. Week after week our relationship grew, and she started opening up and sharing parts of her life. In the big group space, Sydney heard the gospel and gave her life to Jesus. She picked up a Bible and was encouraged to start reading it through an announcement about taking next steps. She loves music and her favorite way to connect with the Lord each week is musical worship. We have grown a lovely relationship over the past five years. We consistently check in and talk each week about ways to follow Jesus. Sydney is a faithful attender of the morning service and a devoted disciple of Jesus.

That's just one example of disciplemaking in the big group space. Sydney's story is not every girl's story in that space, but it is an example of how consistency, program elements, environment, and relationship are helping her become like Jesus.

Big group spaces might not be what we most often think about when it comes to discipleship, but they can be a great launching pad.

LAUNCHING PAD #2: SMALL GROUPS

A caring disciplemaker partnered up with a small group of disciples is an awesome platform to launch relational discipleship with teenage girls. Modeled so clearly for us by Jesus and his twelve, small groups provide a structure that includes modeling, teaching, encouragement, and empowerment. "With is the way," remember? Leaders walking *with* girls to help them become like Jesus. This can happen in different contexts; the key is the number. If it gets too big, it's not a small group anymore. In these groups it's in the smallness that disciplemaking happens.

Environment

- Community/family/friendship vibe
- Consistent space and meeting time
- Ten to twelve girls with two leaders (I think you can go smaller than this, but I don't think you can get any bigger—this is really an ideal size and it's modeled after the way Jesus did it)
- Comfortable seating arranged so everyone can be seen and participate in the conversation
- Safe space where a girl feels comfortable to be herself
- Atmosphere without distractions that promotes conversation
- Launched at designated times during the year
- Find rallying points for girls and leaders to connect to launch these groups. You might want to use the "big spaces," such as camp or a Wednesday night program, as a natural connect point, or have a designated place to register or sign up to participate.

Elements of a small group

- **The first fifteen minutes of group:** Greet and welcome everyone in. Spend time relationship-building and having some intentional fun before you move to structured time. *Bring Uno cards, icebreakers, games, or sports equipment
- **Transition:** Then move from hanging out to a more structured time. Create an atmosphere that sets the tone for conversation, Bible study, practice, and experience.

Disciplemaking with Girls

- **Start the conversation:** Get them talking. Utilize starter questions and intentional icebreakers to give the group permission to share.
- **Show, teach, guide, and empower through conversation:** Choose books of the Bible and intentional content or curriculum to help guide this conversation. Include opportunities to practice and experience the content.
- **Prayer and encouragement:** Share prayer requests and pray together. Give opportunities for girls to pray out loud and pray for one another. Keep a group prayer journal for follow-up and praise reports.
- **Circle back, and close out:** Connect one-on-one with girls you want to circle back with after your conversation.
- **Outside the walls of small group:** Look for ways to share life, make memories, have fun, and build relationships.

Questions to get you thinking

- How will teenage girls connect with a leader in this space?
- How can a girl deepen her relationship with Jesus in this space?
- How will you connect and communicate with parents about this space?
- What resources will you need?

Example

Lexie was invited by a friend to attend a small group. She knew a few of the girls, but she was nervous about joining. She had grown up going to church with her family, but she didn't really know Jesus. After the first few meetings with the small group, she started building genuine friendships with the other girls and had a growing connection with the small group leader. Over the course of a year, Lexie asked a lot of tough questions about God. The small group was a safe place for her to wrestle with big questions and some of the doubts she was having. She showed up every week and by the end of the year felt a closeness and a deep love for the group. She still doesn't have a personal relationship with Jesus, but she is already signed up for the next session. She has two leaders who encouraged her and guided her toward becoming a disciple of Jesus. They created an environment where Lexie felt safe

Creating Rallying Points for Relational Discipleship

enough to be herself and ask her big questions, and they utilized the different program elements to point her to Jesus.

I think it is just a matter of time before Lexie steps into a relationship with her Savior. I am grateful to this small group and the leaders who made space for that to be possible.

LAUNCHING PAD #3: ONE-ON-ONE

One of the ways to make disciples with teenage girls is to meet with them one-on-one. This might be the easiest platform on which to build a discipleship relationship because it is dependent on just a leader and a girl. There are girls out there who can't participate in any other setting, so the option to meet with a caring, godly adult each week could be just the way to help that girl deepen her relationship with Jesus.

Environment

- Warm, welcoming space
- A safe place where both the leader and girl feel comfortable to be themselves (it's wise to consider a public space for one-on-one time with students)
- Consistent location and meeting time
- Atmosphere with limited or no distractions that promotes conversation
- A structure that includes set amounts of weeks/meeting times
- Specific seasonal start times and end times

Elements

- **Checking in and catching up:** Intentional time to open the conversation by talking about life. This is also a great moment to build relationship through having a little fun together. Play cards or bring a game to play to open up the time.
- **Pray together:** Open up your time together in prayer. Check in on any previous prayer requests.
- **Showing, teaching, guiding, and empowering through conversation:** Choose books of the Bible, intentional content, or curriculum to help guide this conversation. Include opportunities to practice and experience the content.

- **Intentional next steps:** How can you encourage a faith next step? Consider serving, Bible reading plan, Scripture memorization, or sharing the gospel with someone.
- **Pray together:** Close your time by praying for one another.
- **Outside the walls of small group:** Find ways to share life, make memories, have fun, and build your relationship.

Example

Casey, a veteran volunteer in our church, met sixteen-year-old Emma while volunteering at our annual Easter services. They were both serving lemonade to people visiting the church for the first time. Who knew a lemonade stand could be a launching pad for relational discipleship? They became fast friends and promised to meet up for coffee. Casey reached out and asked Emma if she wanted to start meeting together for encouragement and prayer. They started meeting for an hour every two weeks at a local coffee shop. What started as a time for connection and prayer turned into a Bible study. They started going through books of the Bible together and spending time talking about God's Word, one chapter at a time. They met for two years and then Emma went off to college as a devoted disciple of Jesus. The one-on-one space is a wonderful customizable launching pad for relational discipleship.

LAST WORDS

Relational discipleship launches from rallying spaces. Girls and leaders need places to meet and begin the journey together. This can happen in so many different ways, from a weekly church service to serving lemonade together. It just takes one moment to launch a relationship that leads to discipleship.

Part Four:
Let's Make Disciples, People!

Disciplemaking with Girls

When I was seventeen years old, I was entrusted with my first group of disciples. We had a Wednesday night youth program that met in someone's home. It started with a short Bible study before we broke into small groups. It was called J.A.M., or "Jesus and me." I am literally giggling and cringing typing that name out. But that was youth ministry in the '90s, people. This was my first experience leading anything. The youth pastor assigned me five girls, and my role was to lead them through the weekly discussion questions and pray with them.

Easy enough, right? Yep, it was. Every week we did the same thing and followed the same rhythm. But what I realized, even as a seventeen-year-old youth worker, is there were a couple of problems with the format. First, the girls had all sorts of questions about their faith and wanted to talk about real things happening in their lives. They were also a little bored. It was tough to continue to engage them when we were doing the same questions every week. That's right: the discussion questions were the exact same every week. Now, I am not criticizing the youth pastor; he had a lot on his plate, and I don't know the reasoning behind what he chose. I also know there are times where repeating the right three questions is effective. But this wasn't one of them.

I wish the end of this story was me telling you I went rogue, wrote my own questions, and that the girls grew in their depth and knowledge under my leadership. But that did not happen. I showed up every week to my circle of five girls and asked the three questions and prayed with them. At seventeen, I just wasn't intuitive enough or spiritually mature enough to know how to do anything else.

I knew back then that there was more to disciplemaking than the discussion questions asked. Good things happened and God moved in that little group. Even though I didn't know what I was doing and it felt boring and unengaging, three of those girls are still walking with Jesus today. I am not patting myself on the back for that, I simply want to point out that there were many things working together in that time to help those girls become devoted disciples. It was a mix of all the ingredients partnered up with God doing his wonderful thing.

Still, I wonder what might have happened if our content had been more thoughtful. How would that have impacted our faith and relationships?

Over the next few pages we are going to unpack how to choose content and how to use content in disciplemaking with teenage girls.

Chapter Fourteen:
Conversations and Content Make Disciples

There is a quote by Maya Angelou that is used often regarding youth ministry: "I've learned that people will forget what you said, people will forget what you did, but people will never forget how you made them feel." Youth ministry people often repeat this quote when talking about the importance of relationships and empathy over content and curriculum in our ministry to teenagers. "They won't remember what you say, but they will remember how you made them feel."

Please don't hate me, Maya, but I agree and disagree with this quote. I agree that the tone and posture in which we communicate to girls is EXTREMELY important and memorable, but I also believe *what we talk about* is really important, too. I think the way we love teenage girls is vital to disciplemaking, but I also believe there is a place to be thoughtful about the content we communicate. Teenage girls remember a lot of what you say, so we need to view content as something that truly contributes to their growth as Christ-followers. The content we present to our girls can actually change their lives, and the spaces we create for conversation can be the difference between a girl who just calls herself a Christian and a girl who is a disciple of Jesus.

If we want to lead girls on an intentional journey to Jesus, then we need to be thoughtful about the content we use to do it.

DETERMINE WHAT THE CONTENT IS GOING TO BE
There are a lot of different ways to define the word "content," but for our purposes together, I am viewing content as anything that helps a girl become like Jesus. Bible studies, devotionals, topical sermons, exegetical teaching, and a hundred other things can be considered

Disciplemaking with Girls

content. Content also comes in many forms: live teaching, paper, digital, video, podcasts, and books, just to name a few. Many forms of content can be part of disciplemaking, but we can't just throw a bunch of content at teenage girls without a thoughtful plan. I want to give you three things to think about when selecting the content you will use with teenage girls.

Choose
There is so much content at our fingertips these days, it's tough to know where to begin. Take the time to be thoughtful about what you choose and why.

Start with prayer
When choosing content for teenage girls the best place to begin is prayer. Ask God what he wants for his girls. Listen for the direction he wants you to go. Follow his lead, and you will find yourself choosing the very best content.

Ask some questions
Before you start looking for content, figure out what you are looking for. Ask questions that will help you narrow down the options and determine the purpose of the content you are going to use.

- Does this help a girl strive to become a devoted disciple of Jesus?
- What are the needs of my girls?
- Where will the content be used?
- Who will be leading/teaching the content?
- What do I want the end result to be for a teenage girl?
- What are the spiritual maturity or growth goals I am hoping to measure?
- How does this content *show, teach, guide, prepare*?
- Does this give girls opportunities for practice and experience?

Create a basic structure
With so many choices out there, creating a basic structure to help with decision-making can make the process less overwhelming. In my youth ministry, I have a simple structure I start with. It's so basic—try not to laugh at me:

1/3 core doctrine/beliefs
1/3 life with and for Jesus (spiritual disciplines, serving, evangelism)
1/3 felt need (what is currently relevant to a teenage girl)

I use these three anchors as the starting points for prayer and decision-making around what content I am going to use in the discipleship of teenage girls. Teenage girls need different kinds of content to help them grow as disciples, so this structure helps me to be thoughtful about a well-rounded scope. The goal is to find a few key pieces that are important to help with your thoughtfulness.

Remember your audience
I know, I know, I have come back to this so many times. But this is CRUCIAL when it comes to content. There is *a lot* of content to wade through. Take the time to really think about and process the content that helps a GIRL love Jesus more and become like him.

Go to trusted sources
Go to places and people you trust to find content. Of course, please be encouraged to create some of your own, but you don't always need to reinvent the wheel. Is there something that already exists that aligns with your ministry vision and your girls? Ask people in your church, in your youth ministry network, or other youth pastors for suggestions.

Plan
Creating a plan for sharing content with teenage girls is a great way to ensure you are being intentional with the journey you are taking her on.

Start with prayer
Yes, again. Do it. Very important.

Think through one calendar year at a time
There are some people who have the ability to do five-year, seven-year, even ten-year plans. I have never been one of them. One year feels like plenty to think about, especially if you are creating a content plan for the first time. I then like to break this year down further by thinking about one season at a time and then one week at a time.

Disciplemaking with Girls

Annually
- Is there an overall goal, vision, purpose, or theme for the content this year?
- What are the start and end points for the content?
- What is the journey we are going to take girls on?
- Are there goals or growth steps we want to measure?

Seasons (summer, fall, winter spring)
- Is there seasonal content you want look for? (Christmas, Easter, etc.)
- Are there any felt needs you want to plan space for?
- Are there times you will want content to create momentum, like after rallying points such as a camp, retreat, or an outreach-type night?
- Do you have any new learnings as a disciple you want to contribute here? Has God put something on your heart that you want to teach or share now?

Weekly
- Who is leading/teaching the content? Are they prepared/equipped?
- Are there any thoughtful practice and experience pieces that need to be added based on this week's content?
- Does the content being shared weekly still align with the overall plan for the year? Are there places to realign?

The following are two content samples from our middle school ministry. As you'll see, we think about the calendar year as whole, but each season is also unique. Things look a little different from year to year, but this is our basic structure.

Conversations and Content Make Disciples

JHM LIFE GROUP SCOPE 2022/2023

SEPTEMBER 2022	
AUG. 30	LG TRAINING, WK. 1
6	LG TRAINING, WK. 2
13/14	LG MEET & GREET
20/21	1ST WEEK OF LG IN HOMES OPTIONS
27/28	OPTIONS

OCTOBER	
4/5	JESUS SERIES (ALIGNED)
11/12	JESUS SERIES (ALIGNED)
18/19	JESUS SERIES (ALIGNED)
25/26	FUN/SERVE NIGHT

NOVEMBER	
1/2	JHM TEAM NIGHT
8/9	6TH: BIBLE; 7TH: BIBLE; 8TH: BIBLE
16	SADDLEBACK NIGHT OF WORSHIP
22/23	(THANKSGIVING)
29/30	6TH: BIBLE; 7TH: BIBLE; 8TH: BIBLE

DECEMBER	
6/7	OPTIONS
13/14	CHRISTMAS PARTIES
20/21	NO LG - CHRISTMAS BREAK
27/28	NO LG - CHRISTMAS BREAK

JANUARY 2023	
3/4	ALL SSM TEAM NIGHT
10/11	DISCIPLINES SERIES (ALIGNED)
17/18	DISCIPLINES SERIES (ALIGNED)
24/25	DISCIPLINES SERIES (ALIGNED)

FEBRUARY	
31/1	FUN/SERVE NIGHT
3-4	LIFE GROUP RETREAT
7/8	6TH: BELONGING; 7TH: IDENTITY; 8TH: PURPOSE
14/15	6TH: BELONGING; 7TH: IDENTITY; 8TH: PURPOSE
21/22	6TH: BELONGING; 7TH: IDENTITY; 8TH: PURPOSE

MARCH	
28/1	JHM TEAM NIGHT
7/8	CONVICTION/SIN SERIES (ALIGNED)
14/15	CONVICTION/SIN SERIES (ALIGNED)
21/22	CONVICTION/SIN SERIES (ALIGNED)
28/29	FUN/SERVE NIGHT

APRIL	
4/5	SPRING BREAK
11/12	OPTIONS
18/19	OPTIONS
25/26	OPTIONS

MAY	
2/3	OPTIONS
9/10	LAST WEEK OF LG OPTIONS
16/17	END OF YEAR CELEBRATION

JHM 2022/2023 WEEKEND SCOPE

JUNE 2022	
4/5	MOVE UP WEEKEND
11/12	LIFE IS BETTER WITH JESUS
18/19	LIFE IS BETTER WITH JESUS
25/26	LIFE IS BETTER WITH JESUS

JULY	
2/3	LIFE IS BETTER WITH JESUS
9/10	LIFE IS BETTER WITH JESUS
16/17	LIFE IS BETTER WITH JESUS
23/24	(CAMP) LIFE IS BETTER WITH JESUS
30/31	(CAMP) LIFE IS BETTER WITH JESUS

AUGUST	
6/7	WE > ME (FRIENDSHIPS)
13/14	SUMMER CELEBRATION WKND
20/21	WE > ME (FRIENDSHIPS)
27/28	WE > ME (FRIENDSHIPS)

SEPTEMBER	
3/4	FALL KICKOFF - YOU BELONG HERE
10/11	YOU BELONG HERE
17/18	YOU BELONG HERE
24/25	ONE-OFF → FELT NEED

OCTOBER	
1/2	CLOSE ENCOUNTERS
8/9	CLOSE ENCOUNTERS
15/16	CLOSE ENCOUNTERS
22/23	CLOSE ENCOUNTERS
29/30	CAMPFIRE STORIES

NOVEMBER	
5/6	CAMPFIRE STORIES
12/13	CAMPFIRE STORIES
19/20	CAMPFIRE STORIES
26/27	ONE-OFF → FELT NEED

DECEMBER	
3/4	IT'S A WONDERFUL LIFE (CHRISTMAS)
10/11	IT'S A WONDERFUL LIFE (CHRISTMAS)
17/18	IT'S A WONDERFUL LIFE (CHRISTMAS)
24/25	NO JHM - CHRISTMAS

JANUARY 2023	
31/1	NO JHM - NEW YEARS
7/8	MIRRORS (IDENTITY)
14/15	MIRRORS (IDENTITY)
21/22	MIRRORS (IDENTITY)
28/29	ONE-OFF → FELT NEED

FEBRUARY	
4/5	GOD'S BIG STORY
11/12	GOD'S BIG STORY
18/19	GOD'S BIG STORY
25/26	GOD'S BIG STORY

MARCH	
4/5	LEGENDARY - TAMAR
11/12	LEGENDARY - RAHAB
18/19	LEGENDARY - RUTH
25/26	LEGENDARY - MARY

APRIL	
1/2	EASTER INTERACTIVE
8/9	NO JHM - EASTER
15/16	THINGS THE BIBLE DIDN'T SAY
22/23	THINGS THE BIBLE DIDN'T SAY
29/30	THINGS THE BIBLE DIDN'T SAY

MAY	
6/7	THINGS THE BIBLE DIDN'T SAY
13/14	JHM PREVIEW WKND → CHANGE
20/21	8TH GRADE WEEKEND
27/28	LAST WORDS WEEKEND

Evaluate

Take time throughout the year to evaluate how the content is working and if it is achieving its goal. This is an important part of determining whether you are on the right track.

Start with prayer
There's definitely a theme here.

Evaluate as you go
Choose a few key times in the year to debrief and evaluate the content. There is no need to continue with content that is not working, is missing the mark, or doesn't line up with the goals you have for teenage

girls. Don't suffer through ineffective content because you are afraid to make a change mid-season or mid-year.

Don't debrief alone
Include the participants in your evaluation. When you debrief the content, be sure to check in with the disciplemakers and the disciples. Their honest feedback might get you to your next best thing.

IMPORTANT THINGS TO THINK ABOUT WITH CONTENT
What do you value?
This is an important area to think through before you choose content or start using it. What do you value for your girls? What components are important to your ministry? What are the non-negotiables? Below are some other questions to get you thinking.

- Do you value a certain translation of the Bible?
- Do you want to emphasize teaching girls to become biblically literate?
- Do you want it to be age-appropriate?
- Do you value a certain format or voice in the conversation?
- Do you want to emphasize an exegetical style?

Don't be afraid to experiment
This is an opportunity to introduce girls to all sorts of ways to grow in their relationship with Jesus. There are so many platforms and avenues to show, teach, guide, and prepare. Mix it up. Try new things. If something doesn't work, you can always tell people, "It was just an experiment."

Age-appropriate
There is a lot of great content out there geared for adults. That doesn't necessarily mean it is also going to be great for teenage girls. Some content can be reworked to be student-friendly, but there is also nothing wrong with girls waiting to engage with that content when they are adults. Remember, this is a journey. There is plenty of time to soak it in at a higher level of maturity.

Let others contribute
Girls and their leaders can be excellent resources for finding

great content. Encourage girls or leaders to share things that have encouraged them in their own discipleship journey. Content from a peer or a leader who is in the middle of the process can be a good starting point for girls in your ministry.

Be a learner
As a disciple yourself, pay attention to all the goodness God is teaching you! Your own journey is a great source of content. What are you learning? What is God showing you? What book of the Bible is blowing your mind right now? Allow the overflow of your own journey to influence content for girls.

CONTENT BEGINS WITH CONVERSATIONS
There are a few ways you can communicate content, but I believe conversation is one of the most effective. Conversation is a cornerstone of discipleship, and it's probably the best avenue for delivering content to a teenage girl.

Conversations are the front door
An intentional conversation opens the door to content. Think of a conversation as a starting point, not the end goal. Becoming a devoted disciple requires more than conversation, but oftentimes conversation is the springboard to moving girls along in their journey.

Conversations help evaluate spiritual maturity
Intentional conversation about the content gives us a picture of where a girl is, how she is processing, and what kind of life change has taken place in her. Conversation around content is a great indicator of what lies ahead in the journey with a teenage girl.

Conversations are the vessel to introducing girls to thoughtful content
Some content is important to talk about, but isn't the easiest subject to broach. I am calling it "thoughtful content," but it could also be called "content that challenges your thinking" or "content that makes you squirm a little." It's good to be thoughtful about teaching or sharing this kind of content through a series of conversations.

    Conversations lead to discovery in God's Word.
    Conversations move toward growth.

Conversations challenge thinking.
Conversations point to Jesus.
Conversations are a way to wrestle with doubt and questions.

LAST WORDS

"They won't remember what you say, but they will remember how you made them feel." I hope that you take away from these pages the importance of our words in the lives of teenage girls. How we make them feel is so important, but our words and the content we choose can have just as much of an impact. The content we present to our girls can actually change their lives, and the spaces we create for conversation can be the difference between a girl who just calls herself a Christian and a girl who is a disciple of Jesus. Whatever you choose when it comes to content, choose it with care and intention.

Chapter Fifteen:
Conversations with Teenage Girls

Recently I got into conversation with some friends who also lead teenage girls. We were swapping ideas and stories. All of us were asking each other, "what kind of conversations are you having with the girls in your group?" and "What content are you using to help them grow closer with Jesus?" Everyone shared a few things they were doing, and we all started taking notes and sending stuff to one another.

There is something so valuable about talking with other women who are leading girls and sharing ideas with each other. Often when you buy a devotional or content or curriculum you are taking a little bit of a risk. You have no idea if it has actually been successful with teenage girls. But when you share and collaborate with people who get it, you know what are using is going to be effective.

This whole chapter is a result of that informal idea-swapping session with my friends. I asked a few of them to share conversations they have led with teenage girls. These conversation guides include language that can be used when a leader is speaking with and leading her group. They can be adapted for large or small settings and can be used in many contexts. I have also included a few of my own favorite conversations.

It would be tough to come all this way together and not leave you with something you could use in your ministry today. My hope is that these conversations will help you lead girls toward a deeper love for Jesus and put them on the path toward becoming devoted disciples.

Disciplemaking with Girls

CONVERSATIONS THAT MAKE DISCIPLES
The following pages include discussion guides on six topics for great conversations to have with girls:
- Scripture memorization
- Biblical identity
- Prayer
- Making wise decisions
- Navigating doubt
- Finding a church after high school

THEME: SCRIPTURE MEMORIZATION

RELATIONAL CONTEXT: One-on-one or small group
Written by Malia Cho, small group leader for five+ years
Used with ninth grade girls
Leaders can use the language below, adapting as needed for their context

THE CONVERSATION
When I was in a small group as a kid (elementary school), there was a huge emphasis on Scripture memorization. Each week when I showed up to group I would recite the memory verse to my leader, who would sign off in my workbook that I did it and add a little sticker to my chart. Once I hit a certain milestone, I could pick a prize out of a toy chest. As I got older, that wasn't part of my small group curriculum, and memorizing Scripture became an afterthought for me.

I think it's so important to memorize Scripture, not just to add a sticker to our progress chart but to help us grow in our faith. Paul tells us in Ephesians to take up the armor of God, and part of the armor is the helmet of salvation and the sword of the Spirit, which is the Word of God. We put on this armor so that we can stand our ground when challenges arise. How do we then make sure we aren't just memorizing the verse but are taking the time to mediate on what it means for us personally? One way to accomplish this is to take it slow, revisiting a list of questions each week and journaling our thoughts. This helps us see if there are any patterns in what stands out to us about a particular verse, and we can notice our growth in understanding.

PRACTICE TOGETHER

The following twelve verses are not the only verses you could or should memorize, but a launching pad to get you started. Pick one verse each week to memorize and spend time meditating on the questions provided.

Memorization suggestions:
- Put the verse to music. Singing and music can act as triggers for memory.
- Read the verse out loud multiple times a day.
- Write the verse on multiple sticky notes and stick them in high-traffic places where you'll see them often.
- Think about the context of the verse. Understanding its overall meaning can help you commit the verse to memory.
- Share the verse with others.
- Meditate on the verse by answering some questions. By taking the time to answer the questions below, you'll plant seeds for these words to take root in your heart and mind.
  o What words or phrases stood out to you?
  o How did you feel reading this verse?
  o How does this apply to my life?

Twelve Starter Verses To Memorize
1. Colossians 2:7
2. Isaiah 43:19
3. Galatians 5:22-23
4. John 14:26
5. Isaiah 9:6
6. Isaiah 40:8
7. Habakkuk 3:18-19
8. Hebrews 10:24-25
9. Psalm 118:1
10. Matthew 28:19-20
11. Hebrews 4:16
12. Ephesians 2:10

Disciplemaking with Girls

THEME: BIBLICAL IDENTITY

RELATIONAL CONTEXT: One-on-one, small group, whole youth group
Emma Aungst, Small group leader for ten-plus years
Used with twelfth grade girls
Leaders can use the language below, adapting as needed for their context

CONTEXT FOR LEADERS
I was discipling a student named Ashley. When we would sit across from each other at coffee or meals, I would see glimmers of confidence outnumbered by lots of insecurity. It broke my heart. During one of our times together God said to me, "I wish she could see herself how I see her." I felt that comment to my core and had the same desire for her. I knew that she was fearfully and wonderfully made (Psalm 139:14) to be uniquely herself. I knew how valuable she is simply because she is a child of God. She didn't. She didn't have a comprehension of her God-given identity and struggled to understand her value. She needed help to build up her biblical identity and to own it.

THE CONVERSATION
Biblical identity is essential to discipleship because as we understand who we were created to be, we get to know our Creator more deeply. Our biblical identity also informs our inherent value. For our relationship with God to flourish, we must see ourselves how he sees us and accept who he created us to be. This is a difficult process because the world's definition of identity and how God would define identity are very different.

QUESTION: When you think of your identity, what comes to mind?

QUESTION: How does the world today define identity?
Leader: The world's definition of identity: who you are, the way you think about yourself, the way you are viewed by the world, and the characteristics that define you.

QUESTION: How does God define identity?
Leader: God's definition of identity: who God says you are, created in his image, made on purpose for his purpose, beloved daughter.

QUESTION: What are the differences between the two definitions?

Leader: We need to keep in mind this reality: If our identity isn't informed by who God says we are, our identity will be formed by the world. The world pressures us to define ourselves through the things we do, financial status, successes, grades, appearance, and what other people say about us, among other things. That is a scary list to find identity in—because what happens to our identity when we experience failure? Or someone doesn't like us anymore? Or we become burned out at school or in our sport? The very foundation of our identity is shaken and altered, resulting in us hustling to define ourselves by something or someone else. A stable identity cannot exist when we base who we are on external things, because that means that when our circumstances change, our identity changes too. When we root our identity in what God says about us, we never scramble or wonder who we are.

PRACTICE TOGETHER

Discover My Biblical Identity
The Bible has a lot to say about our biblical identity. Read through these verses, process the questions, and create the foundation for biblical identity together.

Read Genesis 1:27
What does this say about my identity? (Ex: I'm created in the image of God)

Read Psalm 139:14
What does this say about my identity? (Ex: I'm wonderfully complex)

Read 2 Corinthians 5:17
What does this say about my identity? (Ex: I'm a new person in Christ)

Read Ephesians 3:18-19
What does this say about my identity? (Ex: I am loved by God)

Feel free to add other passages of Scripture that highlight how God sees us or where biblical identity can be discovered.

Creating A Biblical Identity Statement
Use your discussion about the four verses above to create a personal biblical identity statement starting with "I am." The goal is that this personal biblical identity statement would remind a girl of those core Scriptures and help her own her identity.

Disciplemaking with Girls

Example: I am… wonderfully created in the image of God who loves me, made new in Christ, and he has amazing plans for me.

Explore On Your Own

Now that a foundation has been built together, empower your teenager to keep adding to it. Students can spend time in different Scriptures to create an even more robust biblical identity. Encourage girls to read a specific verse a day and think through same question from above: "What does this say about my identity?" Give them the list below as a starting point but leave out the prompts/words (those are for your reference and can be useful in shaping a discussion with a girl). Give them the opportunity to explore identity on their own.

- Ephesians 1:4 (Chosen)
- Deuteronomy 31:6 (Courageous)
- Romans 3:24 (Redeemed)
- Romans 6:6-14 (Free)
- Romans 8:37 (Victorious)
- Galatians 4:7 (Heir)
- Job 33:4 (Valuable)
- Psalms 18:35 (Strong)
- 1 Peter 2:9 (Important)
- Jeremiah 31:3 (Beloved)
- 2 Corinthians 3:12 (Bold)
- Ephesians 2:10 (Masterpiece)

Follow Up

As girls continue to explore and discover their biblical identity in God's Word, check in to ask what God is revealing to them. This can become an ongoing conversation as new pieces are discovered.

THEME: PRAYER

RELATIONAL CONTEXT: Small group
Sandy Oh, small group leader for five-plus years
Used with twelfth grade girls
Leaders can use the language below, adapting as needed for their context

CONTEXT FOR LEADERS
Picture this: You lead a small group of high school girls. It's the end of the night, and you want to end the group time in prayer. You ask if anyone will volunteer to pray and…*crickets.* You look around and everyone is avoiding eye contact with you or making scribbles in their notebooks. After a long silence you call on someone to pray and they reluctantly say yes.

Sound familiar? If not I'm so happy for you, and maybe slightly jealous. The above scenario happens to me on almost a weekly basis. Many of my small group girls feel nervous when asked to pray. They've told me they are worried they aren't going to say the right thing, they might fumble their words, or they might forget a prayer request someone mentioned. Some have said they don't really know how to pray— "What do you mean it's just talking to God?"

CONVERSATION
As Christians, we strive to be like Jesus, and Jesus modeled prayer for us in the Bible. He went off to pray by himself many times,[23] and he taught his followers about prayer, saying that we can present our requests to God and he will hear them and give us what we seek.[24] James 5:16 (NLT) tells us that "the earnest prayer of a righteous person has great power and produces wonderful results." Every relationship requires frequent and honest communication to grow, and our relationship with God is no different.

Prayer doesn't need to follow a structure, but I find it's helpful to have something to start with when you are first establishing the habit. The structure I will be sharing with you is based on an experience I had in college that I really loved.

Disciplemaking with Girls

PRACTICE TOGETHER
When I was in college, we had a conference that included times of prayer. We would break off into groups of three (sometimes with the strangers around us) and take turns praying out loud. One person would pray for our local community, one person would pray for our country, and one person would pray for the world. I call this the "small, medium, large" way to pray because you start with smaller, more personal or specific requests, then get broader.

This is how that structure could look during an average night of small group:
You look at the list of prayer requests and it looks like this: school, tests and projects, club rush, cheer practice, Science Olympiad, hard AP bio unit, and Grandma is sick.

This is how it could look during college application season:
You look at the list of prayer requests and it reads like this: college applications due soon, lots of stress about personal essay for app, worried they haven't done enough, worried their grades aren't good enough.

- **Small:** have one person go through and pray for each individual request.
- **Medium:** have one person pray for the group as they submit applications, and pray for the college admissions counselors as they read through applications.
- **Large:** have one person close out with a reminder that God is in control. We can present our worries to him and trust that he will take care of us.

This method will require you and your students to analyze the requests together and break them down into the small, medium, and large categories. I really love this format because it allows us to see the patterns of our prayer requests over time and stretches us to present our requests in different ways.

Ultimately, I want my small group girls to feel confident when they approach God in prayer. Jesus modeled what it means to present our requests to God while still trusting that his plan is best.[25] I can only hope that by guiding girls to pray in this way during small group they will learn to incorporate prayer more in their daily life.

Conversations with Teenage Girls

THEME: MAKING WISE DECISIONS

RELATIONAL CONTEXT: One on one, small group, whole youth group
*A favorite of Katie Edwards, small group leader for thirty-plus years
Used with high school girls
Leaders can use the language below, adapting as needed for their context*

THE CONVERSATION
Decisions, big and small, can be a bit overwhelming. Often when we are faced with big decisions, we become stressed out or consumed by the decision-making process. But it doesn't have to be that way. God offers a twenty-four-hour support line for all decisions we are faced with. Just kidding, it's not quite like that, but it's close.

God IS available to us daily and there are ways to lean into him while navigating the decision-making process. We do not have to go it alone. But we do have to be intentional about turning to him, seeking his wisdom, and allowing him to lead in our decision-making.

STARTER QUESTIONS
- When you are faced with a big, tough, or life-altering decision, what do you typically do?
- What is your typical process for making a decision?
- Do you ever get stressed or scared or anxious when faced with a big decision? Talk about that.
- How do you typically include God in your decision-making?

Leader note: The categories below are meant to act as a guide for leaning on the Lord in our decision-making. Hearing God's wisdom through his Word. Praying for insight, intervention, clarity, or direction. Talking to wise counsel. Living by listening and then making decisions that honor him.

STUDY TOGETHER
The Bible is probably the most obvious place to find guidance for decision-making, but it's often the last place we turn. If we want God's help and we care about what he has to say, Scripture is a great place to start.

Disciplemaking with Girls

Read Proverbs 2 as a group.

Go to the statements in the passage that have the word "understand/understanding" in them. What are those verses communicating to us?

What promises are made to us when we seek wisdom?
Read through the passage and underline the promises made to us.

PRACTICE
Group activity: Choose someone in the group to share a big decision they are faced with. (If they feel comfortable and safe to share.) Use this decision as a practice scenario to illustrate how to turn to Scripture when making a decision.

Leader note: *Be careful to focus on the biblical process of decision-making, rather than advice on what we would personally do to make this specific decision.*

How can we seek wisdom from God when making this decision? **Start by asking some questions.**

Does the Bible have anything to say about this decision?
Is our particular issue discussed somewhere in the Bible?
Can any insight be gained about our circumstance by looking at the Bible?
Is there someone in the Bible who faced a similar decision?
Is our possible decision consistent with God's Word?

Leader note: *Remember, God will never call us or prompt us to do something that's the opposite of what he's already said.*

SPEND TIME PRAYING FOR A DECISION YOU NEED TO MAKE. ASK GOD FOR HIS INSIGHT, CLARITY, DIRECTION, AND GUIDANCE.
Take a moment and write down a decision you need to make. Now, take a moment and write out what you want to talk to God about with this decision.

Next, pray. Try the simple sample prayer below as a starting point.
Lord, I'm trying to make a decision.
I want to know your thoughts.
I want to make the right choice.
I want to honor you with my decisions.
This is the desire of my heart, but I want to hear from you.
Show me the way, bring clarity, bring next steps.

I trust you and what you have for me.
Be still before God and just listen. Sit in peace and quiet for a minute and wait to hear from him. Be careful not to confuse God's voice with your feelings. What is he saying to you?

SEEK WISE COUNSEL AND ASK FOR INSIGHT, OPINIONS, AND ENCOURAGEMENT.
You are not necessarily looking for answers from others, but you are looking for honest feedback. Coupling what we are hearing from God with the thoughts of God's people helps us to make good decisions.

As a group, create a definition for 'wise counsel'. Write down the names of three people in your life whom you consider to be wise counsel. *(Tip: Look for diversity here: male/female, old/young, friend/family. It's good to have people who love Jesus and are coming from different perspectives to be influencers in your decisions.)*

Leader note: *It's helpful to talk with people who know us, who know our faults and strengths. It's also helpful to speak with a person who knows the situation and may give us a different view on it. But more than anything, it's helpful to find someone who knows the Lord and has been following him for some time. They may not know the "answer," but if they're tuned into God, knowing his heart and ways, this can help us get to the best possible decision.*

As a group, come up with a list of questions you can ask wise counsel when faced with a decision.

LISTEN, COMPILE, AND THEN MAKE THE DECISION!
There will be things that God is asking us to do that make no sense and there will be other things that are simply a decision of preference. God has given us the freedom to choose, so we don't need to seek him for every tiny decision (we'd go nuts!). But it's important to take everything that we learned in the three previous steps and use it before we make important decisions.

Choose a decision you need to make this week and practice the first three steps we talked about. *(Maybe use the decision you wrote down in the prayer step.)*

Compile what you heard God say in Scripture, what you heard in the silence after prayer, and what you heard from wise counsel. Now, ask the questions below:

Disciplemaking with Girls

Is anything rising to the top?
Is there a common theme?
Is a decision being made clear?
Is God leading me a certain way?

Now, make the decision.

THEME: NAVIGATING DOUBT

RELATIONAL CONTEXT: One-on-one, small group
A favorite of Katie Edwards, small group leader for thirty-plus years
Used with tenth grade girls
Leaders can use the language below, adapting as needed for their context

THE CONVERSATION
As humans, we tend to get nervous or scared when we start doubting or questioning what we believe. When we start doubting the things of God or we have questions about our faith, it is easy to feel like we are doing something wrong or dishonoring God. But the opposite is true. You see, we tend to mix up doubt with unbelief. But doubt isn't the opposite of faith; unbelief is the opposite of faith. Doubt is simply a feeling of uncertainty, and it is totally normal and okay to have doubts when it comes to our faith. There are times in our faith and in our relationship with Jesus when we feel strong about what we believe, and then there are times when…well, not so much. Asking questions is a normal and natural part of a growing faith.

Starter question to ask girls: Have you ever experienced doubt in your faith?

STUDY TOGETHER
There is a guy in the Bible named Thomas who had some serious doubts. There are a few things we can learn from him that give us a picture of how to navigate our doubts.

For context: This story happens after Jesus has been crucified and risen from the dead. After that, Jesus appeared to the disciples, but Thomas was not with them at the time. When the other disciples told Thomas about how they had seen Jesus, he didn't believe them.

Read John 20:24-29
Questions to process together:
- Do you think Jesus was upset at Thomas for having doubts?
- What was Jesus's posture toward Thomas?
- What does this moment between Jesus and Thomas tell you about your relationship with Jesus?

PRACTICE TOGETHER
Talk to God about your doubts. It's okay to be honest with him.
Leader: Reassure and encourage students that it is okay to be honest with God about our doubts. Doubting does not mean we are doing something wrong. Keeping doubts hidden without verbalizing them is more damaging than expressing them to God. Only when we are honest and ask questions will we find the truth. God can handle our doubts. Nothing is too big for him to handle.

Ask students to talk about or write down....
- your biggest questions for God
- the current doubts you are wrestling with
- where you need reassurance and reminders from God
- any fears you have connected to doubt

Share your doubts with another follower of Jesus. Don't doubt alone.
Leader: It's important to find a few fellow believers to process doubts with. When we are left processing alone, it is difficult not to let our doubts overtake our thoughts. When we process with someone who loves Jesus, their faith acts as an anchor as we question our own. We can lean into the wisdom and faith of others to help us process the places where we feel uncertain in our relationship with Jesus.

Questions to help students process:
- Who are three people you feel safe enough to share your honest doubts with?
- Where is a safe space for you to process doubts with someone? (if we don't feel comfortable with our surroundings, it will be difficult to open up)
- Who are people you cannot talk with about your doubts?

Say something like: Reach out to the three people you chose and ask them if you have permission to talk to them when you feel doubts creeping in or want to process doubts you are having. Setting this up

Disciplemaking with Girls

ahead of time opens a door in your heart and mind to pursue truth when you are feeling doubt.

Don't live too long in doubt.
Leader: It's okay to have doubts, but doubt is not a place you want to live in too long. Doubts that go unchecked or unquestioned grow. Growing doubt can leave us feeling lost, uncertain, and insecure. When we feel those things, doubts can create false narratives that then have the potential to turn into beliefs.

Create an action plan together of what to do when questions or doubts arise.
For example:
Step 1: Tell God what I am thinking and feeling
Step 2: Call one of my people
Step 3: Explore God's Word

THEME: FINDING A CHURCH AFTER HIGH SCHOOL

RELATIONAL CONTEXT: One-on-one, small group, whole youth group
Created by Nikki Campagna, small group leader for six-plus years
Used with twelfth grade girls
Leaders can use the language below, adapting as needed for their context

CONTEXT
The first time I led a Life Group, I stayed with my girls from the time they started junior high until they graduated from high school. By the time they were seniors, I was a graduating college student myself, and I felt a lot of responsibility for their discipleship process. I wanted to set them up for success in their faith as they were about to step into the season I was finishing.

It's normal for girls to want to try a new church for the new season they are entering (especially if they have grown up at a church). When you partner with your girls in finding a new church, you help them step out to explore, but with a safety net. If we want to see disciples continue to grow after high school, this is something that is worth our time.

THE CONVERSATION
Life after high school can look different for everyone, but one thing

that all teens experience at that stage is transition. Whether they move away for college, stay local, join the workforce, or take time to travel or volunteer, change is inevitable.

I believe that a solid, Jesus-centered community is one of the most important factors when it comes to faith longevity and becoming more like Jesus. Finding a new church to attend after graduating from high school can feel daunting or overwhelming for girls—it's hard to know where to start. Meeting new people and trying out different churches can be a messy process, and it's normal to find it a bit overwhelming.

PRACTICE TOGETHER

Make a list of attributes girls love about their current church so they can look for those things in a new church.
- For example: Is the church involved with the surrounding community? How do they care for people well?
- Encourage your girls to look for "heart" over "vibe." There are a lot of cool churches out there, but what matters more is the heart of the church.
- Talk about the different attributes they wrote down.

Research and enlist help to compile a list of churches to check out. Do a Google search for young adult ministries or college ministries in the area. If a girl is going away to school, search for churches near her new college.
- Check out the website ahead of time to see if the theological beliefs align with what you believe.
- Encourage your student to reach out to the pastor ahead of time and let them know they are going to visit.
- If there is a young adult pastor at your current church, ask if he or she knows of any churches they would recommend in the area where the teen will be living.
- Encourage your students to look for churches that have serving opportunities in ministries they are interested in. For example, if a student wants to lead a small group in the youth ministry, make sure they meet the potential age requirements and the church has a youth ministry.

Visit churches together and then visit on your own.
- If possible, check out a new church together while they are still in high school. This helps you model what it looks like to search for

Disciplemaking with Girls

  a new church and talk about what you liked and disliked after the service.
- Encourage your students to check out new churches with a buddy once they graduate.
- Rule of thumb: Try out a church for three weeks before deciding whether to commit. This will give a fuller picture of a church's culture and overall heart.

Encourage your girls to be all in!
- If a girl is fairly involved at her current church, starting over from scratch at a new church can prove to be challenging. Encourage her to get involved in the church as soon as she can.
- A student will only get as much out of a church or ministry as they put in. In other words, investing in a community will help a girl feel the belonging she is so desperately looking for.
- Go to all the "New People" stuff. If a church has resources or events for first-timers, encourage your student to go, get connected, and take advantage of these things!
- Challenge your girls to step out of their comfort zones and ask one new person at the new church to coffee.
- Remind your students that finding a new church isn't about where they find immediate satisfaction, but where they choose to commit and make a home.

Perhaps most importantly, as girls are searching for a new church home and church family, they need to know they are not alone during what can be an isolating transition. Check in often, pray specifically, and love well.

Chapter Sixteen:
We Get to Do This

When I think about relational discipleship, there is one verse that has always felt like my heartbeat. Do you have one of those? A piece of God's Word whose truth you feel in your bones? The kind of verse that warms your soul and reminds you of why you do what you do? For me that verse is 1 Thessalonians 2:8 (NLT):

> Because we loved you so much, we were delighted to share with you not only the gospel of God but our lives as well.

Paul's words to the Thessalonians here resonate with me on the deepest level. Honestly, they are the perfect picture to encapsulate this entire book. I am chuckling to myself right now thinking about that fact. You could have skipped this whole thing and just read that verse and captured everything you would need to know about discipling teenage girls.

Because we loved you so much.
We shared with you the gospel.
And our lives as well.

This is relational discipleship.
This is what we get to do.

"Because we loved you so much…
    We get to love girls well.
    We get to laugh and cry and listen.
    We get to help girls feel like they belong.

Disciplemaking with Girls

We get to hear the thirty-second stories and thirty-minute stories.

We get to be part of a group chat with sixty-seven text messages.

We get to show up and be present in life's best and toughest moments.

We get to write cards, send encouraging texts, and pray.

We get to show up to school musicals, sporting events and weird extracurriculars.

We get to tell girls how loved they are by God.

We get to remind and reassure them that God loves them just as they are.

We get to tell them they are a beloved daughter of King Jesus.

…we were delighted to share the gospel of God…

We get to point girls to the gospel and the transforming life it offers.

We get to pray with them and for them.

We get to teach them about the richness of Scripture.

We get to wrestle through questions and doubts about belief and faith.

We get to encourage with promises and truth and loving words.

We get guide them toward loving others in the name of Jesus.

We get to pray for their neighbor's dog.

We get to plant seeds in their hearts.

We get to point them to experiences that expand their faith.

We get to participate with them in the body of Christ.

We get to show them how to love Jesus more.

We get to be people who follow and love Jesus in front of them.

… but our lives as well."

We get to invite girls into our lives.

We get to set aside consistent time.

We get to bake or cook or go to the store to buy food for time we'll spend together.

We get to take time to prep content in the car, at the office, or in

We Get to Do This

the parking lot.
We get to sacrifice time with family and friends.
We get to give an extra night or two to disciple girls.
We get to let girls into our homes and, chances are high, clean up afterward.
We get to wait an extra thirty minutes for that one girl to get picked up.
We get to share joys, tough moments, and our story with Jesus.
We are grateful for the time we get to be with our girls.

This is what we get to do.
We get to go and make disciples.
We are ordinary leaders who are called and who get to be part of God's extraordinary story in the hearts of teenage girls.

In the beginning of the book, I called the people who choose to work with teenage girls brave, and I still believe that to be true.

But, after everything we've just talked about, I also just feel honored.

Honored to be invited into what God is doing.

Think about how special it is that Jesus invites us to go and make disciples.

He invites us to be his coworkers in spreading the gospel.

He gives us a front-row seat to life change. Isn't that awesome?

A few things from me to you as you start or continue discipling teenage girls…
You are not too old or too young.
You are cool, even if no girl ever says that to your face.
You are equipped, even if you are not so sure.
You are not alone, God is always with you.
You don't need to have all the answers. Girls don't need you to, either.

Disciplemaking with Girls

You are not in charge. God is always leading and knows where to go.

Your role matters and it is impactful and special.

You don't need to have it all together. In fact it's better if you don't.

You might win some and you might lose some, but God is at work, so that's okay.

You can rest because God never does.

You are never partnered up with a girl by accident.

You are deeply loved by God.

You are a guide and an example to follow and a friend and a teacher.

You are a disciple who makes disciples.

"Your love for one another will prove to the world that you are my disciples."
—John 13:35 (NLT)

Thank you for reading these last words.
I am praying for you as you go and make disciples with teenage girls.
I am standing shoulder to shoulder with you in this crazy time.
I am with you.
And thankfully, God is with us.

Gosh, my heart is so full.

ACKNOWLEDGEMENTS

For the Student Ministries women at Saddleback Church: Emma, Jess, Taylor, Nikki, Jeri, Sandy, Leslie, Megan, Delaney, Stephanie, Brianna, and Toni.
I am truly grateful to have a front row seat to all the ways you shepherd, encourage, and love the girls in our ministry. You are strong, faithful, and wise, and our church is better because of you. It is a privilege to serve with you.

For Malia
Thank you for poring over the pages of this book with me. Your wisdom, discernment, and love for students helped me shape these pages.

For Marko
Thank you for being my cheerleader, mentor, coach, and couch to cry on from time to time. Your belief in me has always meant the world.

For Matt, Jason, Mike, and Bryce
You gave grace, cut slack, and showed up in my absence when I was buried in this project. Chances are high you didn't even realize you were doing it, because that's just who you are. I am so grateful for your unwavering support and ministry partnership. I am humbled that I get to serve with you and learn from you daily.

For Amanda, Emma, Megan, Rob, Kurt, Rachel, Jason, and Stacey
Thank you for being examples of Proverbs 27:17 in my life. You challenge my thinking, you like me at my best and my worst, you encourage me to lean into the fullness of who God created me to be, and I love Jesus more because of your impact on my life. This kind of friendship is a gift beyond what words can express, but I am trying my best to express that *my life is just better because of your friendship*.

For Ron, Abby, Ella & Cooper
Wife and mom are my very favorite roles to play. I feel honored that God chose me to be yours. You are truly the most influential people in my life and loving you is as easy as breathing. Thank you for loving me so deeply and creating space for me to be who God created me to be.

Acknowledgements

And thank you for believing in me beyond what I believe possible for myself. My name might be on the cover, but this, like every other part of my ministry, is always *ours* together.

Disciplemaking with Girls

Endnotes

1. Pauline J. Chang, "Barna Survey: Evangelism Most Effective to Youth." *The Christian Post.* October 13, 2004. https://www.christianpost.com/news/barna-survey-evangelism-most-effective-to-youth.html.
2. Kim Painter, "Teens aren't grasping 'the responsibilities of adulthood', new study says." *USA Today.* September 19, 2017. https://www.usatoday.com/story/news/2017/09/19/teens-grow-up-slower-study/105758486/
3. Barna Group, *Gen Z Vol 2: Caring for Young Souls and Cultivating Resilience* (Ventura, CA: Barna Group, 2021).
4. Barna Group, *Gen Z Vol 2*, page 23.
5. Oxford English Dictionary, "egocentric." OED Online via Google. Oxford University Press, September 2022.
6. World Health Organization, "Adolescent Mental Health." *World Health Organization.* November 17, 2021. https://www.who.int/news-room/fact-sheets/detail/adolescent-mental-health.
7. Barna Group, "State of the Church 2020." 2020. *Barna.* https://www.barna.com/research/changing-state-of-the-church/.
8. Günter Krallmann, *Mentoring for Mission* (Our Generation Publishing, 2014).
9. Sample adapted from document created by Katie Edwards for Saddleback Student Ministries
10. Sample adapted from document created by Katie Edwards for Saddleback Student Ministries
11. Sample adapted from document created by Katie Edwards for Saddleback Student Ministries
12. Adapted from Oxford Languages, "disciple." Accessed via Google, December 2022.
13. Adapted from Oxford Languages, "shepherd." Accessed via Google, December 2022.
14. Adapted from Oxford Languages, "teacher." Accessed via Google, December 2022.
15. Adapted from Oxford Languages, "navigator." Accessed via Google, December 2022.
16. Sample adapted from document created by Katie Edwards for Saddleback Student Ministries
17. Sample adapted from document created by Katie Edwards for Saddleback Student Ministries
18. Sample adapted from document created by Katie Edwards for Saddle-

back Student Ministries
19. Sample adapted from document created by Katie Edwards for Saddleback Student Ministries
20. Oxford Languages, "devotion." Accessed via Google, December 2022.
21. Sample adapted from document created by Katie Edwards for Saddleback Student Ministries
22. Oxford Languages, "meet-cute." Accessed via Google, December 2022.
23. Matt 14:23; Mark 2:35; Luke 5:16, 6:12
24. Luke 11:1-13
25. Matthew 26:36-46